Twayne's United States Authors Series

EDITOR OF THIS VOLUME

Kenneth E. Eble

University of Utah

Herbert Hoover

TUSAS 385

HERBERT HOOVER

By WILTON ECKLEY

Drake University

TWAYNE PUBLISHERS

A DIVISION OF G. K. HALL & CO., BOSTON

Published in 1980 by Twayne Publishers,
A Division of G. K. Hall & Co.
All Rights Reserved

Printed on permanent/durable acid-free paper and bound
in the United States of America

First Printing

Frontispiece photo of Herbert Hoover taken in 1954 at West
Branch, Iowa, appears with the permission of James Kent, the
photographer.

Library of Congress Cataloging in Publication Data

Eckley, Wilton.
Herbert Hoover.

(Twayne's United States authors series ; TUSAS 385)
Bibliography: p. 173–78
Includes index.
1.   Hoover, Herbert, Pres. U.S., 1874–1964—
Literary art.
E802.E25   973.91'6'0924 [B]   80–10686
ISBN 0-8057-7285-5

For Grace and The Boys

Contents

About the Author

Wilton Eckley is Professor of English and Chairman of the Department at Drake University where he has taught since 1965. He has previously taught at Hollins College in Virginia and in Ohio public schools. He received an A.B. degree from Mount Union College (1952), an M.A. degree from the Pennsylvania State University (1955), and the Ph.D. degree from Case Western Reserve University (1965). He was a John Hay Fellow in Humanities at Yale University (1961-1962) and a senior Fulbright lecturer in American literature at the University of Ljubljana in Yugoslavia. Dr. Eckley teaches courses in graduate and undergraduate American literature. He has published *Harriette Arnow* and *T.S. Stribling* for the Twayne United States Authors Series, monographs on e.e. cummings and Bret Harte, and a number of articles on science fiction and the short story.

Preface

Few people, it would seem safe to assume, have ever thought of Herbert Hoover, our thirty-first president, as a writer. More likely than not, most have thought of him, if at all, as the president who caused the Great Depression and then sat and did nothing as the nation suffered through that depression. Be that as it may, Hoover was indeed a writer—and a prolific one at that, with some sixteen books and hundreds of articles, reports, and speeches (the latter which he wrote himself) making up his bibliography. In this so-called "age of anxiety," an age in which flux rather than stability is the rule, Hoover's writings reflect certain human values and social principles that are perhaps worth re-examining.

In several respects one of our more interesting presidents, Hoover led a rich and eventful life—a life that was really many lives woven into one: engineer, millionaire, humanitarian, president, author, and elder statesman. From more-or-less humble beginnings, Hoover rose to the presidency of the United States, only to become a vilified scapegoat for the economic problems besetting the country following the stock market crash of 1929. Unlike the classical tragic hero who falls never to rise again, however, Hoover did live long enough and work hard enough to come out from the closet of disfavor into which he had been thrust, to be received once again by his countrymen as a man of considerable ability and compassion.

Although Hoover the politician and statesman has been the subject of a number of studies—some biased, some objective—no detailed study of Hoover the writer has been done. And it is in his writings (and speeches) that Hoover expressed those principles upon which he predicated his actions. My purpose in *Herbert Hoover* is to examine a selection of Hoover's books and speeches for the light that they shed upon a mind and personality that may be said to be uniquely American. Because it would be impossible to deal with all of Hoover's works in a study of this scope, I have attempted to choose those which bring out most clearly his political, social, and spiritual views.

In order to provide the reader with some background from which to appreciate the works discussed, Chapters 1 and 2 range rather extensively, though certainly not definitively, over Hoover's life. The succeeding chapters cover in essentially a chronological sequence the works in question, beginning with *American Individualism* (1922) and ending with *The Ordeal of Woodrow Wilson* (1958). The final chapter attempts to codify Hoover's ideas as they are reflected in his works and to place Hoover, as a politician, statesman, humanitarian, and thinker, in his rightful place in the American chronicle.

Two major works not treated in their own right in this study are the three volumes of Hoover's *Memoirs* (1951–52) and the four volumes of *An American Epic* (1959–65). Much material from the *Memoirs*, however, does appear throughout; and certainly any student of Hoover would want to read the *Memoirs* in their entirety. They present not only a clear picture of Hoover's thought and action, but also a panoramic view of world affairs as he saw them during his lifetime.

An American Epic presents a definitive picture of the Belgian Relief effort, but is really too specialized and too long to be covered here. But again, the serious student of Hoover would want at least to range through the four volumes to see the tremendous amount of work that Hoover put into it—work that resulted in an informative picture of the economic humanitarianism that was spawned by one of the world's most bloody conflicts. In a very real sense, Hoover is perhaps most at home in the kind of writing reflected in *An American Epic*. This work, moreover, coming as late as it did in his life, shows that Hoover never reached the point where he felt that he had no more to say to the world.

Wilton Eckley

Drake University

Acknowledgments

I am grateful to the Drake University Research Council for a grant to carry out this study; to the excellent staff at the Hoover Library in West Branch, Iowa, for their help and cooperation; to Professor Max Autrey for editorial advice and assistance; to the Herbert Hoover Foundation for permission to quote; and to Mr. James Kent for permission to use his photograph of Hoover.

Chronology

1874 Born, August 10, West Branch, Iowa.
1884 Moves to Oregon, following death of parents.
1895 A.B., Geology, Stanford University.
1897- International mining engineer.
1914
1899 Marries Lou Henry.
1909 *Principles of Mining.*
1912 Publishes translation of Georgius Agricola's *De Re Metallica* (with Lou Henry Hoover).
1914- Chairman, Commission for Relief in Belgium.
1920
1917- Administrator, United States Food Administration.
1920
1918- Member, President's Committee of Economic Advisors,
1919 Paris Peace Conference.
1918- Director-General, American Relief Administration.
1923
1919 Founder, Hoover Institution on War, Revolution, and Peace, Stanford University.
1921- Secretary of Commerce of the United States.
1928
1922 *American Individualism.*
1927 Director, Mississippi Flood Relief.
1928 *The New Day* (campaign speeches of 1928).
1929- Thirty-first President of the United States.
1933
1933 Publishes *Campaign Speeches of 1932* (with Calvin Coolidge).
1934 *The Challenge to Liberty.*
1936- Chairman, Boys' Clubs of America.
1964
1939- Founder, Finnish Relief Fund.
1940

1940–1942	Chairman, Committee on Food for the Small Democracies.
1942	*America's First Crusade; The Problems of Lasting Peace* (with Hugh Gibson).
1944	Lou Henry Hoover dies, January 7.
1945	*The Basis of Lasting Peace* (with Hugh Gibson).
1946–1947	Cofounder, UNICEF; coordinator, food supply for thirty-eight countries in the world famine of 1946–47.
1947–1949	Chairman, Commission on Organization of the Executive Branch of the Government.
1951–1952	*The Memoirs of Herbert Hoover* (three volumes).
1953–1955	Chairman, Commission on Organization of the Executive Branch of the Government (second Commission).
1955–1960	*Addresses Upon the American Road* (eight volumes).
1958	*The Ordeal of Woodrow Wilson.*
1959–1964	*An American Epic* (four volumes).
1964	Dies, October 20, New York City.

CHAPTER 1

Quaker, Engineer, Statesman: Life and Times

TO many of the casual visitors to the birthplace of Herbert Hoover in the picturesque village of West Branch, Iowa, the tiny white-frame cottage, measuring little more than twelve by twenty feet, must seem more a playhouse than a real house that was once home for Jesse Hoover, his wife, Huldah, and their three children, Theodore, Herbert, and May. The cottage, however, was a real enough house for the Hoovers and, as such, symbolizes both the pastoral simplicity and the stark crudity of life in later nineteenth-century Iowa.

Although not a log cabin, the cottage suffices, perhaps, to place Herbert Hoover in that romantic American tradition of the "log-cabin" president—a person who, by his own diligence and perseverance, springs forth from some remote and humble setting to overcome all odds and win the greatest political reward his country can bestow—the presidency. The gap between such origin and such high office has always been of great interest to biographers and readers of biography. Intelligence, ambition, circumstance, timing—all, in one combination or another—have been instrumental in the several cabin-to–White House sagas in the American chronicle. And they were no less so in the career of Herbert Hoover.

I *A Child of the West*

Settled by the Quakers, West Branch, Iowa, on Hoover's birth date of August 10, 1874, was hardly on the cutting edge of the frontier. Yet, in spirit and in life-style it was not far removed. That part of the West was "won" by the time Hoover was born

15

but not yet totally "tamed." It was a place where people were judged not by their background but by their ability to develop a continent. Tillers of the earth, the people around West Branch were indeed de Crèvecoeur's Americans—"cultivators, scattered over an immense territory, communicating with each other by means of good roads and navigable rivers, united by the silken bands of mild government, all respecting the laws, without dreading their power. . .animated with the spirit of an industry which is unfettered and unrestrained, because each person works for himself."[1]

Those with a penchant for romantic nostalgia will, in contemplating West Branch, lean toward the pastoral rather than the crude. Hoover himself stated that he preferred to think of Iowa as he saw it through the eyes of a ten-year-old boy— "eyes filled with the wonders of Iowa's streams and woods, of the mystery of growing crops" and with "adventures and great undertakings, with participation in good and comforting things."[2] Yet life, even for a youngster, was not simply sleigh rides, plunges in the "swimming hole," and hunting excursions with a bow and arrow; there was school, and there was work. "I am no supporter of factory labor for children," writes Hoover in his *Memoirs*, "but I have never joined with the clamor against proper chores for children outside of school hours. And I speak from the common experience of most Iowa children of my day in planting corn, hoeing gardens, learning to milk, sawing wood, and in the other proper and normal occupations for boys. It was a Montessori school in stark reality."[3]

Jesse Hoover was successful enough as a blacksmith that he was able to move his young family to a larger house and to expand his small shop into a farm-implement business that provided a comfortable living. Jesse's life, however, was to be cut short by typhoid fever on December 10, 1880; and Huldah Hoover, with $1,000 of insurance and the proceeds realized from the sale of the implement business, began the frugal life of a widow with three young children. Herbert was now six; his brother Theodore, eleven; and his sister May, four. In order to relieve some of the financial strain on the family budget, Herbert was sent to Pawhuska, Arkansas, to live for awhile with his Uncle Laban Miles, United States Indian Agent to the Osage Indians. He attended the Indian school and, from his classmates, learned much lore of the woods and streams.

Two years later Huldah died of pneumonia, and the family was broken up permanently, with Herbert being taken into the family of another uncle, Allan Hoover, who had a farm close by West Branch. In his recollection of this period of his life, Hoover was impressed with the self-sufficiency of the farmers of early Iowa, whose families were "their own lawyers, labor leaders, engineers, doctors, tailors, dress makers, and beauty parlor artists."[4] In the years following his presidency, Hoover pondered the contrast between such a simple economic system, virtually untouched by the rise and fall of world prices, and the much more complex system brought about by modern technology and marketing practices; for, if any American president felt the meaning of Thomas Jefferson's fears of an industrialized nation, Herbert Hoover surely must have.

The spirit of individualism inculcated in the people of the area around West Branch by the necessity to be self-sufficient, was reinforced from another source—that of religion. Most of the people, including the Hoovers, were Quakers and had inherited not only the conviction that spiritual inspiration sprang from the "inward light" within each individual, but also the idea that religious individualists are inevitably bound together. "The Friends," writes Hoover, "have always held strongly to education, thrift, and individual enterprise. In consequence of plain living and hard work poverty has never been their lot. So far as I know, no member has ever been in jail or on public relief."[5]

Whatever his later views of the Quaker faith, as a child, Hoover found attendance at meetings a rather trying experience. Partly because religious training began early for Quakers and partly because there were no baby-sitters, children from infancy on were brought to the meetings, with the very young being put into the "crying room," off to one side of the meetinghouse. Before he was ten, Hoover had read the Bible through and knew well the patience during long periods of silence at the Sunday meetings waiting for someone to be moved to speak.

But Hoover learned more than patience from his Quaker background. He learned that living was a serious and worthwhile endeavor and that serving mankind was its primary justification. "For the true Quaker," wrote Eugene Lyons in his biography of Hoover, "there is no sharp break between things secular and things sacred; no interval between hardheaded business, let us say, and soft-hearted religion. Worship is not a Sunday soothing syrup for consciences snaggled by weekly necessities. Honest weight and fair dealing figure in Quaker sermons and traditional maxims alongside more abstract principles."[6] A personal religion interpreted by one's own conscience, Quakerism engendered in its followers self-respect, self-reliance, and individual obligation, with the ideal aim of developing "the person not only as an end in itself but as a contribution to the greatest good of the community."[7] In addressing members of the Red Cross on April 12, 1930, Hoover, then president, said, "It is, indeed, the spiritual in the individual and the nation which looks out with keen interest on the well-being of others, forgetful of ourselves, beyond our own preoccupation with our own selfish interests, and gives us a sense of belonging to the great company of mankind, sharing in the great plan of the universe and the definite order which pervades it."[8]

In 1884 Hoover was sent to Newburg, Oregon, a Quaker settlement in the Willamette Valley, to live with an uncle, Dr. Henry John Minthorn, whose own son had died. A country doctor in the classic tradition, Minthorn also taught history and literature at an academy in Newburg; and, like most Quakers, he was a strong believer in education and work. Hoover was steadily exposed to both.

Oregon was a new world for Hoover, one that he found to his liking. The routine of school, chores, and religious exercises kept him busy, but he found time to explore the Oregon forests and streams and to enjoy the typical activities of young boys. Many years later, in answer to a letter from a youngster wanting to know how to become a better citizen, he wrote that beyond knowing and maintaining a government representative of the people, "there are two essentials: first, religious beliefs; second, you should get constructive joy out of life, as you grow up."[9]

In addition to what he got from religion, work, and play, Hoover learned much from Dr. Minthorn, whom he occasionally accompanied on house calls. A veteran of the Civil War, Minthorn was a romantic figure to Hoover and, though usually silent and taciturn, a natural teacher. "He told me much of physiology, health, and sickness," recalled Hoover. "He did it mostly after leaving the patients by way of explosions over the neglects which made them sick. The vigor of his disgust was equaled only by his determination to take no payment from poor non-Quaker families whom he called 'white trash.' "[10] Not a

Quaker who held to extreme pacificism, Minthorn advised
Hoover to "turn your other cheek once, but if he smites it, then
punch him."[11]

After several years, Minthorn opened a Quaker land-settle-
ment business in Salem, and moved his family there. Hoover
worked as officeboy and began to learn of the world of business.
He took advantage of the business college in Salem, particularly
of the interest in youngsters of a teacher who schooled him in
Latin and mathematics. Also an influence on Hoover during this
period was Miss Jenny Gray, who led him into the realm of books,
especially the works of Scott and Dickens. As fast as he would
finish one book, she would bring him another; and he came to see
that though "textbooks are necessary to learning, it was those
other books which stimulated imagination and a better understanding of life. They made the whole world a home. They
broadened my scope and made me feel a part of the mighty
stream of humanity."[12]

Although a few Democrats were present in Salem, the
Quakers, like those in West Branch, were strongly Republican in
their political views. Hoover's interest in public affairs was
whetted when he listened in the evenings to arguments between
these factions over "the various acts of the Arthur, Cleveland
and Harrison administrations, the merits of Jefferson, Lincoln,
Robert E. Lee, U. S. Grant and other statesmen. . . . Free trade
and protectionism always raised high decibles. The debate
invariably ended with complete disgust of each one at the
obstinacy and low intelligence of his opponent."[13]

II *Life at a New University*

When thoughts of a college education for Hoover arose, the
Minthorn family wanted him to enroll at Earlham College in
Indiana, a good Quaker school, but he had other ideas. The field
of engineering had come to look attractive and interesting to
him; and, since Earlham had no engineering program, he argued
that the new university shortly to be opened at Palo Alto,
California, was where he should go. His argument was convinc-
ing; and, with some needed tutoring in several of the non-
mathematical subjects, he passed the entrance examinations and
was enrolled in the first freshman class at Stanford University on
October 1, 1891. Not only was Encina Hall, the men's dormitory

where he lived, to offer him more physical comforts than he had previously known, but the educational experience offered by the university was to start him on the road to being truly an engineer for the world.

At Stanford Hoover developed a close and lasting relationship with Dr. John Branner, head of the Department of Geology and Engineering. Branner was a believer in the basics, grounding his students "strongly in the sciences of mathematics, geology, chemistry, physics, and civil engineering—more strongly than is usual today in our engineering schools. With that equipment, he believed, they would absorb quickly a practical education from their hard knocks. Moreover, so equipped they might shift to any branch of engineering."[14] He recognized in the young Quaker strong qualities of intelligence, integrity, and leadership, and did much not only to teach the fledgling engineer about geology and mining, but also to aid him in obtaining summer work with geological survey parties, from which Hoover gained considerable practical experience. When asked on one occasion why he passed over other apparently qualified students to make Hoover his student assistant, Branner is said to have responded, "Most men fumble jobs, have to be supervised and directed. But I can tell Hoover to do a thing and never think of it again. If I told him to start to Kamchatka tomorrow to bring me back a walrus tooth, I'd never hear of it again until he came back with the tooth. And then I'd ask him how he had done it."[15]

As for his classroom education, Hoover immersed himself not only in the scientific subjects—which came easily enough for him—but also in history, economics, and literature. He found that, although the university had considerable impact upon the more or less fundamentalist religion of the times, his Quaker faith held fairly firm. "I much more easily adapted natural law into my spiritual complex," he said, "than those whose early training was in the more formalistic sects and of wider doctrinal base."[16]

During his senior year at Stanford, Hoover met Lou Henry, a tall, willowy, athletic girl who had been drawn to the university by the reputation of Dr. Branner, who had presented a lecture at her high school in Monterey. She and Hoover met in a laboratory course and soon became attracted to each other. Their courtship, however, was to be interrupted by Hoover's graduation and the three years that Lou Henry still had to complete for her diploma.

Their tacit agreement was that after her graduation and Hoover's establishment as an engineer, they would be married.

III   *Beginning a Career*

Hoover left Stanford in the spring of 1895 with forty dollars and a need for immediate employment. As a result of the financial panic of 1893, the country was experiencing a depression, something that at that time Hoover was not conversant with: "I had lived all my life in hard times. But I never heard of depressions. No one told me that there was one afoot. So I did not need to worry about that. Nor did I have to worry about what the government was going to do about it. No one was crying over 'helpless youth' for that matter."[17] Even at this stage, Herbert Hoover's life view was well on its way to being formed.

To say that Hoover started at the bottom is literally as well as figuratively true. His first job was pushing a car at the lower levels of the Reward gold mine in Nevada for two dollars a day—not impressive, but a start. The Reward, however, cut back its operations after a few months, and Hoover once again was looking for employment. "I learned then," he recalled, "what the bottom levels of real human despair are paved with. That is the ceaseless tramping and ceaseless refusal at the employment office day by day."[18] Perhaps—but when Hoover wrote those words, he was looking back over a number of years and from the position of extensive wealth. He may have felt a need to point out that he himself did understand poverty. One wonders, however, whether a young man of twenty-one, armed with an engineering degree in a growing country, could appreciate the depths of human despair, particularly when his period of unemployment was short.

Through a Stanford connection, Hoover soon obtained a position with Louis Janin, at that time the outstanding mining engineer on the West Coast. After a brief period in the field, Hoover was assigned to the main office in San Francisco at $200 a month. Janin quickly recognized that Hoover was a gifted engineer whose talents would take him far, and he recommended him to Bewick, Moering, an English mining company that was interested in employing western American mining techniques in their gold mines of Australia. The position, paying

$7,500 per year, was that of a consulting engineer for ten mines, some of them located deep in the desolate bush country, where temperatures could be over 100 degrees even at midnight and where water sold for over two cents a gallon. Hoover welcomed the opportunity and accepted the position immediately.

Coolgardie, Australia, where Hoover established his headquarters, lay in the western part of the country, just 300 miles from the sea, and it was indeed desolate. To get to the interior mines, Hoover and his staff rode camels. "I am in a position," he jokingly commented, "to state authoritatively that a camel does not fulfill all the anticipations of romantic literature. He is even a less successful creature than a horse. He needs water oftener than the schoolbooks imply. His motion imparts aches to muscles never hitherto known. No amount of petting will inspire him with affection."[19] Following one of his trips by camel to the interior, Hoover wrote home that he was on his "way back to Coolgardie. Am glad to get back within the borders of civilization. Coolgardie is three yards inside of it. Anybody who envies me my salary can just take my next trip with me, and he will then be contented to be a bank clerk at $3 a week the rest of his life."[20]

Coolgardie was not much different from the typical western American mining camp, though perhaps a bit less "wide open." As one would expect, drinking was prevalent, moving Hoover to comment with regard to the drinking of the Australian and imported Cornish miners that they "had one great virtue in their joy; when they did get solace from the desert in drink, they never seemed to think of shooting up the town; and anyway, they had nothing to shoot with. They ran to sentiment. They'd put their arms around each other's shoulders and sing of Mother."[21] But he could not be so good-natured about other kinds of people that he came into contact with: "I never dreamed such a set of scoundrels could exist as some I have had to deal with. Only yesterday, a man offered me a bribe of $8,000, and on my refusing he tried to place me in a most compromising light. However, I have got him on the wheels now."[22]

One incident that casts some light on Hoover's personality involved an old accountant incapable of carrying on his work that he had to let go. "But when I told him we would need a younger more energetic man," he wrote home, "he broke down and cried, and told me of his wife to whom he sent his entire salary. I have learned he even does his own washing to send her every cent. I am dreadfully put out about it. I have been to see three of our boys. We have made a purse of $300 for him and we think we can get him another place in Perth, that he can fill. . . . If this were my own business, I would be too tender-hearted to let him go; but I have to get things in shape for the company."[23] The above comment shows three characteristics of Hoover, characteristics that are reflected throughout his professional and political life: his sense of compassion, his belief that people should give to help other people, and his unstinting dedication to duty.

As hard as life was in the mines of Australia, Hoover welcomed the challenge and found his experiences both enjoyable and rewarding. His success in Australia was not based on any personal magnetism, for he was not a good conversationalist and talked only with close friends. But he proved himself a man of decision and drive, possessed with a keen ability to analyze a situation and then to take action based on that analysis. Upon Hoover's advice, his company invested $250,000 in a new mining site that proved to be rich in gold deposits, ultimately earning the company over $55 million. Such success gained for him another job offer—a similar post in China with the Chinese Engineering and Mining Company, a large business owned primarily by Chinese but managed by Europeans, including Bewick, Moering. He eagerly accepted the post and just as eagerly cabled Lou Henry with a proposal of marriage, a proposal that was a classic example of the brevity with which Hoover carried on his correspondence: "Will you marry me?" The answer, just as brief, was "Yes."

IV *Engineering for the World*

Hoover and Lou Henry were married in Monterey. Because there was no Quaker meeting in that area and no Protestant minister in the town, they were married by Father Ramon Mestres, a Catholic priest, in Lou Henry's home on February 10, 1899. The next month they were on their way to China to set up housekeeping in Tientsin, from which base Hoover made extensive trips to the interior, learning firsthand much about Chinese life and government. These trips also provided him with ample time for reading—Chinese history, Confucius, Mencius, economics, sociology, Plato, Shakespeare, Schiller, and Goethe, among other things. Mrs. Hoover, too, was learning much about Chinese life, and in later years she was to recall the period in China as one of the happiest of her life.

The lives of the young couple, however, were suddenly interrupted by the Boxer Rebellion, the avowed purpose of which was to drive all foreigners from Chinese soil. On Sunday, June 10, 1910, Tientsin was bombarded by Boxer artillery and laid siege to by 25,000 troops. The American, Japanese, German, French, British, Russian, and Italian soldiers stationed in the city were greatly outnumbered. The ranking officer, a Russian colonel, called upon Hoover to use his engineering ability to fortify the city as best he could with what was available. The latter enlisted both foreigners and Chinese to construct barricades from sacks of sugar, peanuts, and rice around the exposed areas of Tientsin. Over 60,000 shells were fired into the city during the siege, but the embattled group held out until relief arrived one month later.

Many years after, a group of Hoover's political backers prepared a press release describing his activities during the siege of Tientsin, focusing particularly on a true incident in which he rescued a child trapped in the line of gunfire. 'They made the tactical mistake," wrote Eugene Lyons, "of showing the text to Hoover before releasing it. He read the story, frowned, slowly tore the sheets into the tiniest fragments, and dropped them into a waste basket. 'You can't make a Teddy Roosevelt out of me,' he said quietly in a way that foreclosed argument."[24]

Following the Boxer Rebellion, Hoover was instrumental in reorganizing the Chinese Engineering and Mining Company, a complex and difficult task, considering the chaotic state of China at the time. His experiences during this period led him to an impression of "abiding admiration" for the Chinese people. Patient and tolerant, they were, in Hoover's mind, temperamentally at a disadvantage in competing with militaristic races: "Indeed the militaristic races to the north of them have furnished nearly every dynasty over 3,000 years. And the people have absorbed every conquering northern tribe and made it Chinese. The inflexible mores of the race will inevitably absorb any conquest of them."[25] He saw the Chinese as less mechanically minded than Europeans and basically poor administrators—this latter factor militating against any democratization of China.

In the fall of 1901, Hoover was offered a junior partnership in
Bewick, Moering. He accepted, and at the age of twenty-seven
he moved with Mrs. Hoover to London. The company did
business all over the world—from Nevada to South Africa—
necessitating considerable traveling for Hoover and providing
for contacts, with, as he put it, "leaders of men, heads of
governments, and public officials; with snobs and crooks; with
plain, good people and intellectually inspiring people, with
human boll weevils."[26] Between 1901 and 1908, Hoover covered
in his travels, most more than once, the United States, France,
Australia, New Zealand, Canada, India, Hawaii, Egypt, Italy,
Malay, Burma, China, and South Africa. "There was," he said,
"good food and bad food, there were good beds, bad beds, bugs,
mosquitoes, dust, sand, and malaria. There were the excitements
of dealing with officials decent or dumb, of passenger stories
pointed or dull, of glorious scenery, of soft tropic mornings at sea,
of freezing northern storms, of strange peoples and customs, and
finally of arrivals and custom officers. There was daily meed of
joy and sorrow."[27]

Mrs. Hoover accompanied her husband on many of his trips,
even after the arrival of babies. Herbert, Jr., was born on August
4, 1902, and five weeks later the Hoovers were enroute to
Australia with the infant in a basket—prompting Hoover later to
remark that "traveling with babies is easier than with most
adults."[28]

With some hope of spending more time in the United States,
Hoover in 1908 left Bewick, Moering and set up a new
engineering organization with offices in New York, San Francisco, London, Petrograd, and Paris. The idea was to serve as
"engineering doctors" to various sick concerns that, with
competent management, could be made once more profitable.
"Ours was a happy shop," said Hoover. "There was the sheer joy
of creating productive enterprises, of giving jobs to men and
women, of fighting against the whims of nature and of correcting
perversities and the incompetence of men."[29]

As involved as he was in "correcting the perversities and
incompetence of men," Hoover found time to do his first writing
for publication. Along with Mrs. Hoover, he translated from the
Latin Agricola's *De Re Metallica,* a sixteenth-century folio on
engineering. In 1909 he published a small engineering textbook
entitled *Principles of Mining,* which was, as he described it in the

preface, "a condensation of a series of lectures delivered in part at Stanford and Columbia Universities. It is intended neither for those wholly ignorant of mining, nor for those long experienced in the profession."[30] In twenty chapters the book ranges from mine evaluation and development to the character and obligation of the mining engineer, the latter serving as another indication of Hoover's view that business and duty go together. "There is now demanded of the mining specialist," he says, "a wide knowledge of certain branches of civil, mechanical, electrical, and chemical engineering, geology, economics, the humanities. . .and in addition to all this, engineering sense, executive ability, business experience, and financial insight."[31] Engineering sense, to Hoover, was made up of honesty, ingenuity, and intuition. His approach to engineering problems consisted of five steps: (1) determination of the value of the project, (2) determination of the method of attack, (3) detailed delineation of method, means, and tools, (4) the execution of the works, and (5) the operation of the completed works. He was to follow these steps basically in any problem he encountered in his life, mining or not.

By this time, Hoover's engineering career had brought him considerable wealth; but, even more significant perhaps, it had taken him to many regions of the world and afforded him the opportunities to acquire a keen interest in, and a valuable knowledge of many peoples of the world—interest and knowledge that were to be reflected significantly in his later endeavors as statesman and author. He saw, for example, that although to many Americans "Europe consists of magnificent cities, historic cathedrals, art, music, literature, great universities, monuments of human heroism and progress," under its "400,000,000 people of a score of races lie the explosive forces of nationalism, of imperialism, religious antagonism, age-old hates, memories of deep wrongs, revenges, fierce distrusts, repellent fears and dangerous poverty."[32] His years in England permitted him a firsthand view of English society, a society which, despite the liberal progress attributed to it, was to Hoover one far behind America in terms of many essential social actions, e.g., free education, restraint of monopolies, control of child labor, old-age pensions. He saw America as having begun the struggle against the evils of the industrial revolution much earlier than England.

Among the opportunities for being an engineering doctor were several in Russia, and Hoover made a number of lengthy visits to that country in the six years prior to World War I. Particularly interesting in terms of the microcosms it presented of all of Russia was Kyshtim estate in the Ural Mountains, an estate of 1.5 million acres that supported farming, mining, and industry. Here Hoover learned much about what he referred to as the "tragedy of Russia": the great chasm between the noble family at the top of the social and economic structure and the 100,000 peasants and workers at the bottom, a picture of which came to him "one day upon a railway station platform, where a long line of intelligent decent people brutally chained together were marched aboard a freight car bound for Siberia. Some were the faces of despair itself, some of despondency itself, some of defiance itself."[33] Hoover was so struck by this scene that he suffered recurring nightmares about it and knew that before long the country would undergo a violent explosion.

Preceding the explosion Hoover could see coming in Russia, however, was one detonated in Sarajevo, Bosnia, on June 28, 1914, with the assassination of Archduke Francis Ferdinand, heir to the throne of Austria-Hungary. Hoover, like many others at the time, hoped that war could be averted. He wondered what implications the tense situation held for his world-wide enterprises. Events moved rapidly, and in little over a month the world was indeed at war. Though he may not have realized it at the time, Hoover's career as a mining engineer was over. He was about to embark on another kind of engineering career—one that ultimately would carry him to the presidency of the United States.

V   *A New Kind of Engineering*

Robert Skinner, the American consul in London, was under considerable pressure to aid stranded American tourists, who, because the advent of war had closed the banks, could not cash checks. He called upon Hoover, who immediately got together as much cash as he could and helped Skinner cash small checks for the tourists until the money ran out. The American embassy in London was under even more pressure, and Ambassador Walter Hines Page prevailed upon Hoover to direct a program to help the thousands of Americans descending upon London in an effort

to find ship passage home. The Hoovers put off their plans to
return to the United States, and both of them went to work to set
up the program. With the Savoy Hotel as headquarters, Hoover
enlisted the aid of five of his American engineers. After a hectic
month and a half of work, they had the task essentially
completed; and the Hoovers once more looked forward to
returning to California.

Because of his efficient handling of the refugee program,
however, Hoover was asked to take on another task: the feeding
of millions of starving Belgians, whose food had been seized by
the invading Germans and whose ports were closed by the Allied
blockade. Asking for a day to consider the request, Hoover
returned to his London house to ponder his future. Mrs. Hoover
and the boys had already departed for America. It took three
days for him to make his decision. Will Irwin, who was staying
with Hoover at the time, explained Hoover's quandary as having
been one of not whether he should go to the aid of the Belgians,
but one of whether he should try to keep a hold on his potentially
lucrative business affairs. Were he to do so, he knew that Europeans would accuse him of seeking concessions and advantages
for his own interests. "On the fourth morning," reported Irwin,
"he came down to breakfast with his accustomed mien—
pleasantly sober. We were alone in the dining room. He bade me
good morning, poured and sweetened his coffee, looked up
and—'Well, let the fortune go to hell,' he said."[34]

Hoover divested himself entirely of any responsibility for, and
remuneration from, his business interests, and took over the
Commission for Relief in Belgium. His assumption then, like that
of most people, was that the war would be over in less than a
year and that the Belgians would be all right after the next
harvest. "The knowledge that we would have to go on for four
years, to find a billion dollars, to transport five million tons of
concentrated food, to administer rationing, price controls,
agricultural production, to contend with combatant governments
and with world shortages of food and ships, was mercifully
hidden from us. I did not know it but this was to be not only a
great charity to the destitute, but it was the first Food
Administration of a whole nation in history."[35]

Probably no more appropriate person could have been found
to head the Belgian Relief than Hoover. To him, a problem was a
problem; and providing food to a starving nation was not

basically different from developing and operating mines. As the *World's Work*, in a biographical sketch, commented on the choice of an engineer for such a task, "those who know the basic commerical industry of mining have no illusions as to what constitutes greatness in that calling. The leaders are the generals in an efficient and delicately organized industrial army which produces the second of the world's greatest primary commodities—the minerals."[36] Hoover was now involved in delivering the first of the world's greatest primary commodities—food.

Hoover quickly put his organization together, calling upon five of his top engineering executives and two members of the press to serve as directors of the program. He put himself in charge of international diplomacy and fund raising and soon became a familiar figure in various capitals of Europe. On his first trip into Belgium, he "had an indescribable feeling of entering a land of imprisonment. . . . German soldiers stood at every crossroads and every street corner. The depressed, unsmiling faces of the Belgians matched the mood of the dreary winter landscape. There were no children at play. The empty streets, the gaunt destroyed houses, the ruins of the fine old church of St. Pierre and the Library of Louvain, intensified the sense of suspended animation in the life of a people."[37] Here indeed was a result of total war.

In a visit to Germany, it came to Hoover that the Germans were really the Spartans of Europe, reviving, consciously or unconsciously, the ancient Spartan concept of total war. The seriousness and efficiency with which the Germans had mobilized an entire population to the task of fighting a war gave Hoover grave doubt as to whether the British and the French could overcome their fumbling approaches to the war soon enough to prevent a German victory. "In any event," he said, "I came back with the complete conviction that the war would not 'be over in the spring'; in fact with the belief it had not yet really begun."[38]

Hoover had a chance to see the war firsthand in 1916 when, while in Germany negotiating for the Belgian Relief, he was invited by a German colonel to view the Battle of the Somme from a German observation post. The sight was a shocking documentation to Hoover's aversion to war: "Seen through powerful glasses, in the distant view lay the unending blur of trenches, of volcanic explosions of dust which filled the air

where over a length of sixty miles a million and a half men were
fighting and dying."[39] Hoover saw the lines of German wounded
returning from the battle "in the silence of sodden resignation."
It was with such vivid scenes in his mind that he hoped fervently
that President Woodrow Wilson would succeed in keeping the
United States neutral. But when he returned in 1917 to America
to seek more money for the Belgian Relief, he saw that emotion
had taken over from reason and that the idea of a war as a war to
preserve democracy "was accepted despite the incongruity that
victory would cement the Czarist regime upon the Russian
people."[40] The irony involved here with regard to the final effect
on Russia of the war is obvious.

VI *Back to America*

With America's entry into the war, President Wilson prevailed
upon Hoover to return to Washington to become United States
Food Administrator. Hoover agreed, with the stipulation that he
continue in charge of the Belgian Food Relief and that he receive
no remuneration. He felt that "the position would carry more
moral leadership if I were a volunteer alongside of my
countrymen in war."[41] He also convinced Wilson that the best
organizational procedure was not to set up a board, but to focus
the power in a single individual to be titled Administrator. This
was to be the only war agency not under a board or a commission.
Hoover's theory was that he could function more effectively and
efficiently without the inevitable "frictions, indecision, and
delays" inherent in the control of an impersonal board. As he
stated at one of the early staff meetings in answer to why there
was to be no organizational chart, "this is an emergency
organization and a new operation. Every day we must meet new
problems. Therefore, my notion on organization is to size up the
problem, send for the best man or woman in the country who has
the 'know how,' give him a room, table, chair, pencil, paper and
wastebasket—and the injunction to get other people to help and
then solve it. When that problem is out of the way, we shall find
plenty more."[42]

Hoover was warmly heartened by the positive response of the
American people to the Food Administration and saw in it a
confirmation of his belief in the strong moral character

engendered in the typical American by the democratic tradition inherent in the country's development. "We found in the American people," he remarked, "exactly what we expected—a wealth of cooperation. Saving food became a sort of game. Parents took advantage of it to impose upon their children the disciplines which had been the griefs of their own youth—and blamed it on me."[43] The motto was "Go back to simple food, simple clothes, simple pleasures. Pray hard, work hard, sleep hard, and play hard. Do it all courageously and cheerfully. We have a victory to win."[44]

Hoover believed that democracy's foundation lay in the individual initiative of its people and that, when faced with an emergency, such people will rally to the cause and leave selfishness and self-interest behind. Voluntary action was the key, because it would preclude the necessity for "Prussianizing" America; and it would, he later was to maintain, stand as a bulwark against the new threat to freedom that was spawned by the war—communism.

VII *The Aftermath of War*

Europe at the Armistice was a shambles; and America's aid was again needed, this time to save the Continent from the "flames of starvation, pestilence, revolution, and to start the rebuilding of industry and life."[45] Hoover was asked by President Wilson to transform the Food Administration into a new agency of relief and reconstruction for Europe. With Alonzo Taylor, Robert Taft, Julius Barnes, and Lewis Strauss, Hoover sailed for Europe on November 17, 1918. As a group, they were full of optimism: "There would be a period of great difficulties and readjustments but the new spirit of men that had carried the war would carry the peace and reconstruction. The purification of men, the triumph of democracy would bring a new golden age."[46]

As far as Hoover was concerned, the optimism was rather shortlived. In a meeting in London with Allied representatives to discuss programs and organizations, he found that although the English, the French, and the Italians were idealists as individuals, they were something else when viewing their own nation's problems. Empire was foremost in all of their minds. Hoover's reaction was to shunt power politics aside, leaving it to bureaucrats, and attend to the problems of starvation and reconstruction. "The American people," he postulated, "did not require the permission of anybody to undertake this second intervention in Europe."[47]

One of Hoover's primary concerns was the vast number of orphaned children in every town and city of the liberated and enemy areas. These millions of undernourished and diseased children touched Hoover's humanitarian impulses, certainly, but they also gave him grave practical concern. Unless they could be helped quickly, "their distorted minds were a menace to all mankind." Indeed, "there were many beyond full repair and these were one of the origins of the brutes who made the Second World War."[48]

As usual, his approach to this problem was pragmatic: he took advantage of the universal love of children, for it seemed to him "that around this devotion there could be built a renaissance of unity of hope among their distracted leaders. I hoped that in this evidence of someone's concern for their children there might be a lessening of the consuming hates that burned in the hearts of women because their own children or millions of the children of their nation had come to this condition."[49] Thus, another example of that interesting mixture of humanitarianism and pragmatism that so often marked Hoover's career. He even viewed the results of the child-feeding program quite pragmatically when he wrote in a letter to President Wilson that "the reaction which I receive from all over Europe indicates that we have touched the heart of the populations at large as much by this child feeding department as in any form of American intervention in Europe. Its continuation for some months will, in my mind, contribute to smooth out their ruffled feelings which are bound to arise from the polical settlements."[50]

To the great consternation of the British and French and even some Americans, Hoover also worked to open the door for food to Germany. His justification for such aid to a former enemy came in a prepared statement in which he listed one pragmatic argument after another for such action, closing with the forward-looking point that "we and our children must live with these seventy million Germans. No matter how deeply we may feel at the present moment, our vision must stretch over the next hundred years and we must write now into history such acts as

will stand creditably in the minds of our grandchildren."[51]
Maintaining the blockade on Germany from the Armistice in
December till late March 1919 did much, in Hoover's mind, to
implant a bitterness and a burning desire for revenge in the
German mind that was to boil to the surface in a short time and
lead the world once more into total war.

VIII   *Efforts toward Peace*

Because of his knowledge of the situation in Europe, Hoover
played a significant role in the peace negotiations. While not a
member of the five-man American peace mission, he had rooms
with them at the Hotel Crillon and "dealt," as he put it, "with the
gaunt realities which prowled outside" the formal discussions.[52]
He did serve on a number of the committees of the peace
delegation and was called upon frequently by the four Allied
leaders—Wilson, Clemenceau, Lloyd George, and Orlando—for
information and advice. He viewed his mission as not only the
nourishing of millions of destitute people, but also the shielding
of "the frail plants of democracy in Europe against the withering
blasts of the time and their possible aftermaths of unemployment, anarchy, or Communism."[53] The third pitfall was the one
he feared most; the first two would merely lead to it.

But solving the peace puzzle was in its own way just as
perplexing as was the winning of the war. Woodrow Wilson may
have been acclaimed as a kind of savior by many Europeans
when he arrived on the Continent, but he soon faced the stark
realities of jealousy and vengence, of hatred and fear, that
marked the struggle for peace—realities that Hoover had been
dealing with for four years. Firm believer that he was in
American idealism, Hoover knew that it was out of place in the
diplomatic intrigues of Europe; and he reminded Wilson that it
would be folly to be dragged into political and economic areas
where America had no interests.[54] Maintaining an "independence
of action" was paramount for America in Hoover's view, for only
in that way could she be an effective moral force in the world.
"In my view," he wrote, "if the Allies cannot be brought to adopt
peace on the basis of the 14 points [Wilson's plan], we should
retire from Europe lock, stock, and barrel, but we should lend to
the whole world our economic and moral strength, or the world

will swim in a sea of misery and disaster worse than the dark ages."[55]

When, early on the morning of May 7, 1919, Hoover was awakened by a messenger delivering to him a draft of the peace treaty to be presented later that day to the Germans, he was greatly disturbed at what he saw as hate and revenge running through the political and economic sections. The conditions demanded were not, in his mind, conducive to rebuilding a Europe of peace. Walking the Paris streets at dawn that day, he met General Jan Smuts and John Maynard Keynes, who also saw grave consequences stemming from the treaty as it was written. Referred to as the "Puck of Economics" by Lloyd George, Keynes agreed with Hoover regarding the economic conditions being laid before the Germans. Keynes later remarked that "Mr. Hoover was the only man who emerged from the ordeal of Paris with an enhanced reputation. This complex personality, with his habitual air of weary Titan (or, as others might put it, of exhausted prize fighter), his eyes steadily fixed on the true and essential facts of the European situation, imported into the Councils of Paris, when he took part in them, precisely that atmosphere of reality, knowledge, magnanimity, and disinterestedness which, if they had been found in other quarters, also, would have given us the Good Peace."[56]

Along with some others, Hoover called upon Wilson to discuss the treaty; but the president's physical condition bordered on exhaustion, and he became irritated with some of Hoover's direct remarks. Hoover drew up a rather lengthy memorandum on the subject of the treaty, and a copy was sent to Wilson. After reading it, the president sent for Hoover. In the course of their meeting, Hoover once again aroused Wilson's ire: "I had, perhaps, used over-vigorous words. He flashed angrily at these expressions as being personal accusations against him—which I, least of all persons, had never intended. But his nerves, like those of all of us, were taut. Colonel House had already broken with him over the Treaty and left Paris. Other than a formal goodby at the railway platform at Paris, I never saw him again while he was in the Presidency."[57]

When Hoover left for the United States in September, a little over two months after the signing of the peace treaty, he carried with him the conviction that America might win wars but it could never make a lasting peace. It should, therefore, remain neutral in Old World wars, work to prevent war, and, in the wake of war, attempt to heal the subsequent wounds. He was to examine the matter in *The Problems of Lasting Peace* (1943), a book written in collaboration with his friend Hugh Gibson.

CHAPTER 2

An American Hero

AFTER five years of concern with the problems of war, Hoover was eager to get back to California, to get out the fishing gear, to live again—and, above all, "to renew association with a great lady and two highly satisfactory boys."[1] Not yet forty-five, he had hopes of resurrecting his engineering career and opened offices in San Francisco and New York. Popularity and national acclaim, however, prevented him from reverting to the role of engineer and family man—a role that he really did not want, anyway. He had gone beyond that. Selected by a *New York Times* poll as one of the ten most important living Americans, in the months from October 1919 to March 1921 he gave out thirty-one press statements, wrote twenty-eight magazine articles, made forty-six public addresses, presided over fifteen public meetings, gave evidence at nine congressional hearings, and made four extensive reports on various subjects. He had reason to feel that he "had adopted a Pullman berth as my eternal home."[2]

Although his nonpartisan stance during the war had precluded any real standing in either political party, a number of Hoover's friends began to work for his nomination as a candidate for president in the coming 1920 election. He was a registered Republican, but he had loyally served a Democratic president. He was indeed an example of, and a believer in, the two-party system, feeling that each party had its unique strengths and weaknesses. His name was placed in a number of primaries, some on the Democratic slate and some on the Republican, though he tried to prevent such from occurring wherever he could. The one exception was California, where he made a strong showing against U.S. Senator Hiram Johnson, garnering 210,000 votes against 370,000 for Johnson.

I   *Into the Political Arena*

With the election of Warren G. Harding, Hoover became Secretary of Commerce, serving in that post for more than seven years, until the middle of 1928, when he ran for president on the Republican ticket. He was particularly pleased with this position in the cabinet because he knew that there was much to do in the areas of development and reconstruction of the nation's foreign and domestic commerce. The Department of Commerce might have been next to the bottom at Washington dinner tables, but it was foremost in Hoover's mind and in the unflagging energy he devoted to it—still holding to the principle of never accepting any remuneration for public service.

Hoover saw Harding as a man with a dual personality, genial and pleasing, but lacking the experience and intellectual quality demanded by the presidency. The two worked well together, however, and Harding often listened to, and followed, Hoover's advice. On a trip by boat to Alaska, a few days out, Harding asked Hoover whether, if he knew of a great scandal in the administration, he would expose it or bury it. Hoover's response was to expose it and at least get credit for integrity. The scandal in question, of course, was the infamous Tea Pot Dome episode. On the return trip, Harding suffered a heart attack and heart specialists were called to meet the party at the Palace Hotel in San Francisco. Another massive attack, however, took the president's life. "Warren Harding," Hoover was to state after he himself became president, "had a dim realization that he had been betrayed by a few of the men whom he had trusted, by men who he had believed were his devoted friends. It was later proved in the courts of the land that these men had betrayed not alone the friendship and trust of their staunch and loyal friend but they had betrayed their country. That was the tragedy of the life of Warren Harding."[3]

Hoover had only a passing acquaintance with Calvin Coolidge, the new president, but he saw him as being "well equipped by education, experience, and moral courage for the Presidency."[4] Particularly was he impressed by Coolidge's New England "horse sense" and the Puritan rigidities which, in Hoover's mind, served the nation well. The only caveat that Hoover held regarding Coolidge was the latter's reluctance to take any action in advance of pending trouble, with the result that he was unprepared for the trouble if and when it arrived. An example was the rising boom and wild speculation beginning in 1927, in which, though urged by Hoover and others to take some action, he did nothing—thus ultimately bringing on the Black Thursday of 1929.

When Coolidge announced on August 2, 1927, his intention not to run for reelection in 1928, a considerable number of hopefuls began jockeying for position. Hoover, too, was under heavy pressure to enter the race. As early as 1920, both Democrats and Republicans thought him to be of presidential caliber, but he chose to bide his time. "While I deeply appreciate the many fine things that have been said of me," he stated at that time, "I do hope it will be agreed that I am so constituted that I am not neutral on much of anything of importance. Yet, as I must maintain my independence until I can see the definite party alignment and the nomination of men on the great issues before the country, my friends will recognize that the application of political machinery to myself is impossible."[5] This time, however, Hoover decided to try at least to "apply" political machinery to himself. He won the Republican nomination easily on the first ballot—and tasted momentarily a political glory that was to be all too fleeting.

Hoover was confident that, barring any mistakes, he would win the election. Prosperity—no small ally—was on his side, and he could easily have sidestepped any serious debating of issues. Yet he felt it necessary to take advantage of the campaign opportunity to attempt to educate the voters regarding the major issues facing the nation, and he did so with only seven major addresses.

No great differences distinguished Hoover from Alfred Smith as they carried on a campaign of the highest levels of sportsmanship and ethics. "No word," wrote Hoover of the campaign, "had been spoken or misrepresentation made by either of us which prevented sincere friendship the day after election."[6] He could not, however, say the same for the lower rank and file of party workers on either side—he himself being the victim of some mud-slinging regarding his engineering and business practices in China and California and Smith being the target of a number of attacks by religious bigots.

The aspersions cast upon himself Hoover saw as "merely run-of-the-mine incidents typical of any American political campaign. Any man entering public life knows that gremlins of this sort will eventually tear at his public reputation"[7]—an ironic understatement indeed when viewed in light of the smear campaign that was to follow him during, and long after, his administration. The religious attacks upon Smith, however, upset Hoover considerably, for they struck at what he perceived to be the very essence of the American spirit: "In this land, dedicated to tolerance, we still find outbreaks of intolerance. I come of Quaker stock. My ancestors were persecuted for their beliefs. Here they sought and found religious freedom. By blood and conviction I stand for religious tolerance both in act and in spirit. The glory of our American ideals is the right of every man to worship God according to the dictates of his own conscience."[8]

Hoover won the election by some 6 million popular votes and by 375 electoral votes and began one of the more ill-fated administrations in American political history.

II *Road to Depression and Defeat*

Hoover recognized that over the years the power of the office of president had risen in almost direct correlation to that of the United States itself, gaining in ascendancy over the legislative branch. As a symbol to the nation, the president is seen as having even more responsibility for the national welfare than in reality he has and "in the end," according to Hoover, "has become increasingly the depository of all national ills, especially if things go wrong."[9]

Feeling somewhat hampered in his inaugural address because he was succeeding a president of his own party, Hoover confined his comments to the ideals and aspirations of America, speaking about better law enforcement, the relations of government to business, and world peace and disarmament—concluding,

The government must, so far as lies within its proper powers, give leadership to the realization of these ideals and to the fruition of these aspirations. No one can adequately reduce these things of the spirit to phrases or to a catalogue of definitions. We do know what the attainments of these ideals should be: the preservation of self-government and its full foundations in local government; the perfection of justice whether in economic or in social fields; the maintenance of ordered liberty; the denial of domination by any group or class; the building up and preservation of equality of opportunity; the stimulation of initiative and individulity; absolute integrity in public affairs; the choice of officials for fitness to office, the direction of economic progress toward prosperity and the further lessening of poverty; the freedom of public opinion; the sustaining of education and of the advancement of knowledge; the growth of religious spirit and the tolerance of all faiths; the strengthening of the home; the advancement of peace.

There is no short road to the realization of these aspirations. Ill-considered remedies for our faults bring only penalties after them. But if we hold the faith of the men in our mighty past who created these ideals, we shall leave them heightened and strengthened for our children.[10]

Hoover's program was to be three-directional: continuing the reconstruction and development measures he had been involved with as Secretary of Commerce; encouraging and working toward reforms in the nation's social and business life; and reorienting foreign relations toward greater cooperation for the advancement of peace and international progress. Certainly a worthy program. As Hoover was soon to discern, however, circumstances were to prevent him from even getting it off the ground. "But instead of being able to devote my four years wholly to these programs," he lamented, "I was to be overtaken by the economic hurricane which sprang from the delayed consequences of the World War. Then the first need was economic recovery and employment. And some actions otherwise possible would have retarded recovery."[11] Nevertheless, he was able to do some things in such areas as water resources, commercial aviation, housing, and child welfare.

For two years prior to his election, Hoover had been concerned about the rampant speculation in the stock market. His warnings to investors, though, were not heeded; and the nation moved with carefree abandon toward the day of reckoning. That day, of course, was Thursday, October 24, 1929—when the stock market dramatically began its inexorable slide into the valley of depression. Before it was to end, banks were to close, businesses were to fail, homes and farms were to be lost—and whatever talents for organization and problem-solving Hoover had were to be sorely tested.

In the eyes of many, these talents were deemed lacking. Indeed, the Depression has often been referred to as the "Hoover Depression," with the implication being that not only was he himself the cause of it, but also that he did nothing to end it. Anyone with the slightest knowledge of economics would agree that the cause of the Depression can be traced to events and patterns that were too complex and too long in coming to be laid at the feet of one man, president or not. As for what Hoover did to combat the downward economic slide, we must remember that he had no precedents to guide him. Moreover, he truly believed that the Depression would be shortlived and that the underlying strength of the American economy would make itself manifest and reverse the then current trend. The specific challenge as Hoover saw it was to take corrective steps that would not inflict upon the country a collectivist economy, and thus destroy the personal liberty to which it was dedicated.

Despite his fear of the specter of collectivism, Hoover knew that the government would have to take upon itself a new role, using existing powers and obtaining more, as needed, from Congress. At the same time, however, he was not about to encourage the government to jump into risky social and economic experimentation that might, in the end, undercut the spirit of American individualism in which he so strongly believed.

After finally consenting to Reconstruction Finance loans to states for relief purposes, he said, "For the first time in history, the Federal government has taken an extensive and positive part in mitigating the effects of depression and expediting recovery. I have conceived that if we would preserve our democracy this leadership must take the part not of organizing dictatorship but of cooperation in the constructive forces of the community and of stimulating every element of initiative and self-reliance in the country."[12]

One of the most urgent tasks that Hoover faced was to restore some semblance of confidence in the people that it was not the end of the American social and political system. To dispel any such fears, Hoover gave a number of addresses during his four-year term emphasizing the essential soundness of the American system and the moral strength and ingenuity of the American people. In a speech at Valley Forge on May 30, 1931, he pointed out that Washington and his troops met the challenge of cold and starvation and emerged in the end triumphant: "If those few thousand men endured that long winter of privation and suffering, humiliated by the despair of their countrymen, and deprived of support save their own indomitable will, yet held their countrymen to the faith, and by that holding held fast the freedom of America, what right have we to be of little faith?"[13]

As economic bad news began to sweep over the ocean from Europe in the spring of 1931, the demands for more government action grew stronger, mixed with cries for socialistic or fascistic remedies. Hoover's response was that turning to a state-controlled social or economic system would be to replace democracy with tyranny under the guise of liberalism. That the government should use its power to provide leadership and initiative, Hoover did not question. But he insisted that responsibility be shared by states, communities, and individuals, and that governmental programs "should be set up in such form that, once the emergency is passed, they can and must be demobilized and withdrawn, leaving our governmental, economic, and social structure strong and wholesome."[14]

Hoover felt that one of the main problems he faced in trying to pull the nation out of the slough of depression was the lack of cooperation from a Democratic Congress. He declined to battle publicly with Congress in favor of doing his best "to cooperate, consult, explain, and implore, with the hope of getting somewhere."[15] He felt no president had the right to undermine the independence of the legislative branch of government: "The constitutional division of powers is the bastion of our liberties and was not designed as a battleground to display the prowess of Presidents. They just have to work with the material that God— and the voters—have given them."[16]

And working with that material was not one of Hoover's strong points. As Thomas S. Barclay, who knew Hoover personally, explained, "it hurt him politically that he was not able to adjust to the practice of American politics in dealing with Congress. He was used to having an organiztion that he controlled and directed. . .with a very loyal staff, but you can direct Congress only to a certain point."[17] There is little doubt that Hoover would have liked to have had the kind of free hand he demanded when he took over the Belgian Relief and the Food Administration under Woodrow Wilson; but, alas, there was no one to give it to him.

The Depression reached bottom in July 1932, with some 12.4

million unemployed; and Hoover, supported by a number of independent analysts, maintained that recovery was underway. Still, he knew that there was little hope for reelection in the fall. Prosperity helped him in 1928, and depression was hurting him in 1932. This fact he could accept, but he could not accept what he felt to be the extremely unfair tactics the National Democratic Committee followed. He characterized those tactics as four years of personal attack orchestrated by John J. Raskob, Chairman of the Democratic National Committee; Jouett Shouse, Executive Director; and Charles Michelson, Publicity Director.

In addition to efforts by the Democratic organization to discredit Hoover and his policies, there appeared a number of "smear" books depicting Hoover as not only inept, but self-serving and conniving. One such was *The Strange Career of Mr. Hoover* by John Hamill, who purported that all the material in his book could be documented. Under threat of a suit for libel, however, Hamill confessed that he had fabricated the entire book.

The Bonus March on Washington in July, 1932, by World War I veterans, provided another avenue of attack against Hoover. These veterans were demonstrating in hopes of obtaining from Congress action to pay a deferred war bonus in cash instead of over a period of years. Hoover opposed such action, as did the majority in Congress. When it became evident that no action on the matter was forthcoming from Congress, Hoover obtained funds to buy tickets home for the demonstrators. Some 6,000 took advantage of such aid and left. About 5,000 remained—a group described by Hoover as "mixed hoodlums, ex-convicts, Communists, and a minority of veterans."[18] There is some room for belief that Hoover was describing this group more as he would have liked to have seen them than as they actually were. Either way, when police asked them to leave an old building they were occupying, fighting broke out, and two marchers were killed. Hoover ordered General Douglas MacArthur to remove the remaining demonstrators and to restore order. MacArthur carried out the order, and the Bonus March was over. For Hoover, however, it was a no-win situation; he was accused during the 1932 campaign as being calloused and insensitive to human rights and human suffering.

The campaign of 1932 was fought primarily on the depression

issue, with Roosevelt blaming Hoover for causing the Depression and then for doing nothing to alleviate its effects and Hoover vainly trying to explain and justify his actions or inactions. This campaign will be discussed more fully in Chapter 4.

The election was really no contest. Franklin D. Roosevelt won easily; the nation got its New Deal. A bitter pill, certainly, for Hoover; but, as he later remarked, "democracy is not a polite employer. The only way out of elective office is to get sick or die or get kicked out. Otherwise one is subject to the charge of being a coward, afraid to face the electorate."[19] In his last address as president, he summed up his view of government service:

We are but transitory officials in government whose duty is to keep the channels clear and to strengthen and extend their dikes. What counts toward the honor of public officials is that they sustain the national ideals upon which are patterned the design of these channels of progress and the construction of these dikes of safety. What is said in this or in that political campaign counts no more than the sound of the cheerful ripples or the angry whirls of the stream. What matters is— that God help the man or the group who breaks down these dikes, who diverts these channels to selfish ends. These waters will drown him or them in a tragedy that will spread over a thousand years.[20]

III   A Revolution Back to Personal Freedom

With the giving up of almost forty years of administrative responsibility and nineteen years of government service, there came for Hoover "a great sense of release. It was emancipation from a sort of peonage—a revolution back to personal freedom."[21]

Personal freedom for Hoover, however, meant opportunity for work. In his concern for the revitalization of the Republican party, he cast himself in the role of the loyal opposition to the New Deal administration. His first effort was a reexamination of those convictions upon which he had based his public life, resulting in the publication of *The Challenge to Liberty* (1935), a work to be discussed in detail in Chapter 5. Following that book came almost a dozen other books, numerous articles, and hundreds of speeches, as Hoover continued his career on what he called the American Road.

Hoover's attacks on the New Deal gave rise to speculation that he might again run for president, and his stirring speech to the 1936 Republican Convention in Cleveland increased that speculation. "Republicans and fellow Americans," he exhorted, "this is your call. . .lead the attack to retake, recapture, and remain the citadel of liberty. . . ."[22] Such speculation, however, was groundless; and the Republicans, still wary of the earlier attacks on Hoover, nominated Alfred M. Landon. Disappointed though he must have been, Hoover campaigned strenuously for the unsuccessful Landon.

In 1938 Hoover traveled once more to Europe to enjoy the honors and plaudits bestowed upon him by a continent still grateful for his humanitarianism during and following World War I. He even had a forty-minute interview with Adolph Hitler.

War clouds once again hung heavy over Europe; and, upon his return home, Hoover spoke out strongly against American involvement in any European conflict. In 1939 he wrote a small book entitled *Shall We Send Our Youth to War?* It examines the difference between his feelings toward America's involvement in World War I and those toward her involvement in the latest conflict. War to him was not something good and glorious, but something evil and devastating—something which every effort should be made to avoid. Even as one by one European nations were attacked by Germany, Hoover remained steadfast in his neutral position. "The immense task now," he said to the Republican National Convention in Philadelphia in 1940, "is to shape our foreign policies to protect us from the conflagration in Europe and Asia. . . . The most vital realism in our relations with the world today requires that we keep out of wars unless the Western hemisphere is attacked."[23]

With the Japanese attack upon Pearl Harbor, Hoover saw no choice but to accept the task of fighting and defeating the enemy. "I have believed," he said, "that alternative policies would have been better. But whatever our differences of view may be as to the causes which have led to this situation, those are matters to be threshed out by history. Today there is just one job before the American people. We must defeat this invasion by Japan and we must fight it in any place that will defeat it."[24]

Although victory in the war was America's first task, Hoover saw another task of equal significance: the problem of achieving

a lasting peace. It was to this end that he and Hugh Gibson wrote
The Problems of Lasting Peace (1942) and its short sequel *The
Basis of Lasting Peace* (1943).

On January 7, 1944, Lou Henry Hoover died of heart failure in
the Hoover apartment at the Waldorf Astoria in New York,
bringing to a close a marriage of deep love and unstinting loyalty.
"I had lived," wrote Hoover, "with loyalty and tender affection
of an indomitable soul almost fifty years. Hers were those
qualities which make a real lady: loyalty and gentle consideration for the rights and needs of others, no matter who."[25]

In some respects, ex-presidents are awkward for a country to
have around, particularly when the "ex-" is of a different
political persuasion from the party in power. Throughout
Roosevelt's administration, he and Hoover traded jibes at each
other; and Roosevelt would give Hoover no official tasks in
helping to win the war. For a man who thrived on work, this was
truly a frustrating situation. With the end of the war, however,
President Harry Truman asked Hoover to use his talents in
making a world-wide survey of food needs. Hoover, of course,
was eager to do what he could and, with Hugh Gibson and a team
of experts, set out on an extensive trip in 1945 to assay the
world's food situation. While his job this time was primarily that
of fact-finding, he did exert some influence in the handling of the
world food problem. During this same period, he became a
cofounder of UNICEF (1946), another example of his serving the
peoples of the world.

Hoover's last official duty for the government was heading two
commissions to study the bureaucratic functions of the national
government, the first in 1947–1949, the second 1953–1955.
These commissions became known as the Hoover Commissions.
While their reports and proposals drew generally favorable
comment from various segments of government and press, they
seem to have had little, if any, lasting impact on the way big
government functions. For Hoover himself, however, they
served as a kind of tonic. Senator George D. Aikin of Vermont,
regarding the effect on Hoover of his activities on the
commissions, said, ". . .I think simply the injustices that had
been committed against him had really affected his health. . . .
As the two years of study went on, you never saw anyone recover
his health as fast as Herbert Hoover did."[26]

Hoover lived out his remaining years in relative quiet as an elder statesman, enjoying a deserved rise in reputation as the nation seemed, in retrospect, to gain a clearer understanding and appreciation of the principles upon which he based his personal and political life. During this period, he continued speaking and writing—publishing a number of books and articles—until his death on October 20, 1964.

CHAPTER 3

The Divine Spark of Individualism

CENTRAL to Herbert Hoover's life view was his concept of individualism and his unswerving belief that America was to stand as an inspirational example to herself and to the rest of the world of the positive power of such individualism in assuring the freedom and dignity of mankind. Ironically, that concept of individualism was the key to both his success as a statesman and humanitarian and to his failure as a politician. It might well be said that Herbert Hoover was born too late, that the ideal he espoused was, like Jay Gatsby's, lost somewhere in the past of the Republic and that to hold on to it in modern times was indeed ignoring the forces of history. Perhaps so, but the fact remains that to understand the basic motivations of Hoover, we must come to terms with what he so often referred to as American individualism.

In 1922, while Secretary of Commerce, Hoover set down his ideas of individualism in a small book titled simply *American Individualism*. His principal desire at the time was, as his assistant Edgar Rickard wrote in a letter to Howard J. Heinz, "to get it into the hands of people who need a simply expressed sermon bringing to their minds the cause of the various upheavals which worry all of us today."[1] The publishers, Doubleday, Page, heralded it as a "book that may be as important as a battle." And surely Hoover himself saw it as a kind of battle—a battle in a war that he waged through his entire career against what he saw as the debilitating and perhaps even fatal influences that threatened individual freedom.

I *Why American Individualism?*

When he was writing *American Individualism*, World War I was still fresh in the mind of Herbert Hoover. His firsthand
48

experience in dealing with the suffering and hunger of millions of dispossessed civilians had left an indelible impression. To be sure, he had known some aspects of want in his earlier years, but not the kind he saw in Europe during and after the war. For the victims of the war, there was no available road to self-betterment, no real possibility of finding, through determination and hard work, a way out of the tight circle of deprivation into which they had been cast. They sorely needed the help that the United States, under Hoover's direction, provided. But Hoover was realist enough to know that beyond the humanitarian motivation for such aid lay a cogent practical motivation—the fear of revolution; and he acknowledges this fear in the opening sentence of *American Individualism:* "We have witnessed in this last eight years the spread of revolution over one-third of the world."[2]

Hoover recognized, moreover, that the war itself was much more than the result of a combination of virulent nationalism and diplomatic misunderstandings and blunderings. It was, in the broader spectrum of the evolution of civilization, an explosion whose causes "lay in the great inequalities and injustices of centuries."[3] Implied in his comment here seems to be the idea that the war was inevitable and that even if the apparent reasons for its ignition in 1914 could have been dealt with nonviolently, other ostensible causes would eventually have arisen to set it off. Despite his original hopes that America, at least, would stay out of the war, Hoover was not unaware that once violence is let loose in the world, it breeds more violence—and very often revolution. For from the turbulence of war often come "dreamers" with theories and formulas that promise to solve all human troubles.

Even if such theories and formulas do not foment violent revolution, they can foster considerable unrest and discontent with what Hoover calls "the surer forces of human advancement."[4] Following the high hopes for the betterment of civilization engendered in espousing noble causes in a war often comes disillusionment as the problems of peace prove to be as difficult as those of war. Hoover's involvement in the peace efforts following the war made him keenly aware of this irony. And herein lay his purpose for writing *American Individualism.*

Like the able engineer that he was, Hoover thought it vital to get to the root of a problem, to strip away the superfluous foliage; for only when a problem is truly recognized can efforts be made toward solving it. And this, he says, is the task of America: to define clearly those "political, economic, and spiritual principles through which our country has steadily grown in usefulness and greatness, not only to preserve them from being fouled by false notions, but more importantly that we may guide ourselves in the road of progress."[5] *American Individualism* was designed to aid in this task.

II   *The Challenge to Individualism*

Hoover points to a number of social philosophies that were, in the period following the war, contending with each other— American individualism, European individualism (in the more democratic countries), communism, socialism, syndicalism, capitalism, and autocracy. These philosophies, he says, "are in ferment today in every country in the world. They fluctuate in ascendency with times and places. They compromise with each other in daily reaction on governments and Peoples."[6] He does not argue the merits of these philosophies one against another, nor does he deny that one may be more adaptable to a particular nation or race. What he is concerned with primarily is "their challenge to the physical and spiritual forces of America."[7] He recognizes, moreover, that there are those even in America who are advocating a turning away from the traditional social values that have been the keystone in America's development in favor of a newer social scheme.

Vivid phrases and catchwords, Hoover warns, are dangerous because of their power to stir people to precipitate and unthinking actions. Demagogues use them to excuse hate and destruction in the name of political idealism. What Hoover fails to realize here is that virtually any ideal, even his own American individualism, is expressed more often than not through catchwords, phrases, and slogans. Indeed, we might turn through the pages of *American Individualism* and construct a fairly long list of such catchwords and phrases.

Hoover himself, however, expresses no doubt regarding the authenticity and vitality of his brand of individualism. The truth of it, he says, "has been confirmed and deepened by the searching experiences of seven years of service in the backwash and misery of war. Seven years of contending with economic degeneration, with social disintegration, with incessant political dislocation, with all of its seething and ferment of individual and class conflict, could but impress me with the primary motivation of social forces, and the necessity for broader thought upon their great issues to humanity. And from it all I emerge an individualist—an unashamed individualist."[8] How much like Walt Whitman's "I" of "Song of Myself"—an egoistic comic hero moving confidently and resolutely through an ordered cosmos, one who will take us by the hand, lead us to a new identity, and prepare us for the challenge of life.

III   The Nature of American Individualism

Hoover leaves no doubt that he views his individualism as a uniquely American individualism, for it is in America that the concept of individualism has realized its greatest advancement. Its uniqueness lies in the ideals that Hoover sees it embracing: "that while we build our society upon the attainment of the individual, we shall safeguard to every individual an equality of opportunity to take that position in the community to which his intelligence, character, ability and ambition entitle him; that we keep the social solution free from frozen strata of classes; that we shall stimulate effort of each individual to achievement; that through an enlarging sense of responsibility and understanding we shall assist him to this attainment; while he in turn must stand up to the emery wheel of competition."[9]

Such ideals place a premium on individual achievement and recognize, moreover, a reciprocal responsibility between society and the individual to insure this achievement. The key element—one that tempers a life view that might otherwise become excessively harsh and inflexible—is equality of opportunity. While Hoover was not so naive as to believe that all men are created equal in terms of intelligence, character, ability, and ambition, neither was he a believer in social Darwinism nor in the eighteenth-century idea of laissez faire—"the notion that it is every man for himself and the devil take the hindmost."[10]

His own life, of course, was all Hoover needed to document his theory of equal opportunity. He had seized the opportunity afforded him and had risen from a humble background to a position of wealth and leadership. If he could do it, so could others. All they had to do was to measure up to the "emery wheel of competition."

Hoover's "emery wheel" metaphor may to some seem simply another way of expressing the laissez-faire policy which he so carefully rejects in *American Individualism*. Like Jefferson, Hoover sees nothing inherently wrong with competitive economic relationships in which wealth is distributed on the basis of ability and ambition. The paradox arising from such a view is the same for Hoover as it was for Jefferson: equality in law and equality of opportunity are not the same, no matter how neatly such an equation can be theoretically stated. How, for example, are we to know when the devil has taken, or is about to take, the hindmost?

It is not unusual, of course, for there to be a gap between a man's theory and his practice. Nevertheless, what becomes at least partially clear is the difficulty that Hoover had throughout his career of reconciling the strong element of self-reliance in his life view with that of a genuine concern for the hindmost; for they were both essential parts of his makeup. The solution, as he sees it in *American Individualism*, is to embrace the idea of service and responsibility to others. Only then can individualism ward off the social injustice that, under whatever guise, could destroy not only it, but the free society for which it serves as a cornerstone.

Hoover declines to attach a neat label to the social system that evolved in America, fearing perhaps that a specific label would in some way circumscribe or devitalize the robust spirit that he sees underlaying the fabric of that system. Implied in a label is the assumption that certain groups or individuals will dominate others; and such an assumption, in Hoover's view, would be anethema to the social force that he sees as being superior to socialism, capitalism, syndicalism, or any other "ism." For American individualism "is far higher and far more precious a thing than all these. It springs from something infinitely more enduring; it springs from the one source of human progress—that each individual shall be given the chance and stimulation for development of the best with which he has been endowed in heart and mind."[11] Juxtaposed against the Old World ideas of individualism, then, American individualism proves itself more vigorous, more dynamic—indeed, more transcendental.

When Hoover states that individualism is not merely a stimulus to production and the road to liberty, but "alone admits the universal divine inspiration of every human soul,"[12] he echoes the views of the two leading American exponents of individualism, Ralph Waldo Emerson and Walt Whitman. Like Emerson, he sees the soul as the essential source of individualism; and, with Emerson, he would agree that "each eye was placed where one ray should fall, that it might testify of that particular ray."[13] Like Whitman, he sees the need to reconcile the assertion of the singleness of man—of individualism—with concern for the mass, because only from the latter "comes the other, comes the chance for individualism."[14] Neither Whitman nor Hoover sees the problem of reconciliation as insoluble, though they both see it as difficult. Both recognize that in individualism is the threat that it will preclude a necessary broader social perspective.

Hoover addresses himself much more directly to this problem than does Whitman, realizing that individualism, at the same time that it works to free the energies of creativity and production, must also exert a limiting force. It must control and direct in positive paths the "inherited instincts of self-preservation, acquisitiveness, fear, kindness, hate, curiosity, desire for self-expression, for power, for adulation, that we carry over from a thousand generations."[15] Hoover was never the totally naive optimist in his estimation of mankind. Selfishness was real to him; he had seen it operate in various ways all over the world. Yet, his basic position was optimistic, for he felt that selfishness could be restrained while the finer impulses of man were encouraged. Thus he can say in *American Individualism* that "the most potent force in society is its ideals."[16]

This division of man's makeup between selfish instincts and idealistic impulses places Hoover not only in a Quaker context, but also in a Platonic one: "With the growth of ideals through education, with the higher realization of freedom, of justice, of humanity, of service, the selfish impulses become less and less dominant, and if we ever reach the millennium, they will disappear in the aspirations and satisfactions of pure altruism."[17] Yet he could see that self-interest was, for the foreseeable future, a necessary force for mans survival; for without preservation, there can be no progress. He recognizes that of "the impulses that carry us forward, none is so potent for progress as the yearning for self-expression, the desire for the creation of something. . . . Here lies the great constructive urge

of mankind. But it can only thrive in a society where the
individual has the liberty and stimulation to achieve."[18]

IV   The Economics of Individualism

Having established that the base of American individualism is
spiritual, Hoover has no problem in shifting from the ideal to the
practical. He believed that theory without practice was worth-
less and that "high and increasing standards of living and comfort
should be the first of considerations in public mind and in
government. . . ."[19] No further justification for such a priority is
needed than the realization that increasing the standard of living
for a people is advancing the civilization of that people. Unlike
Emerson, Hoover easily blends the spiritual and the material into
a smooth and logical mix.

Indeed, the impulse to production and the stimulation to
invention are at the base of individualism in that they not only
derive impetus from it, but also provide nourishment to it. And it
is precisely on this point that socialism fails—because it denies
the individual impulse to create or to achieve in favor of an
economic and social structure imposed from above.

American individualism, however, must not be viewed simply
as an economic creed with its only end the acquisition and
preservation of private property; for property is nothing more
than an instrument to stimulate initiative on the part of the
individual—"not only stimulation to him that he may gain
personal comfort, security in life, protection to his family, but
also because individual accumulation and ownership is a basis of
selection to leadership in administration of the tools of industry
and commerce."[20] Interestingly enough, then, we are left with
the idea that the means are more significant than the end; that is,
those processes (industry and commerce) used to acquire
property really become an end in themselves.

Hoover has no fear that capital will ever become an oppressor
in America. The American demand for equality of opportunity
will serve as a safeguard that no group will ever assemble enough
property to control the government. Along with this rather
idealistic belief, he points out that individual ownership is
becoming a thing of the past, giving way to corporate ownership

made up of the aggregated small savings of many people. He believes that from such community ownership will come morality in the business world.

Even though Hoover defends such a view with the practical argument that "masses of capital can only find their market for service or production to great numbers of the same kind of people that they employ and they must therefore maintain confidence in their public responsibilities in order to retain their customers,"[21] it is difficult to accept his position as being anything other than naive. The acceptance of a pragmatic base for moral action moves individualism a considerable distance from the spiritual mooring that Hoover talks about earlier. He does admit the possibility that such groups as chambers of commerce, trade associations, labor unions, farmers, and others can develop warring interests that may lead them to try to dominate the government and thus threaten the foundation of individualism. But, at the same time, he sees the greater possibility that a "sense of service, a growing sense of responsibility, and the sense of constructive opposition to domination, constantly recall in them their responsibilities as well as their privileges."[22]

In the movement of business toward more and greater cooperation, Hoover sees the potential for even greater growth of individualism. He sees such cooperation not as a movement in the direction of socialism, but as a blend of the initiative of self-interest and a sense of service. "Their only success," he says, "lies where they eliminate waste either in production or distribution—and they can do neither if they destroy individual initiative."[23] This phase of the development of individualism he sees as the dominant force in the expansion of the twentieth century.

Hoover recognizes that with the shift from an agrarian society to one based on industry and commerce, there have arisen tremendous challenges to America's ability to keep malign forces from destroying the matrix of individualism and freedom. But he feels that America has answered these challenges and in so doing has proved that individualism is not a static concept, but one that is ever able to evolve in the arena of social, economic, and intellectual progress.

V   The Politics of Individualism

In discussing the political aspects of American individualism, Hoover points to two schools of thought regarding government: "one that all human ills can be cured by governmental regulation, and the other that all regulation is a sin."[24] From these neatly drawn polarities, he proceeds to lay much of the responsibility for the discontent with the functioning of government to World War I. By its very nature, war impinges upon individualism and would ultimately destroy it. American government, however, has been more successful than most in upholding individualism and equality before the law: "It has gone the greatest distance of any government toward maintaining an equality of franchise; an equality of entrance to public office, and government by the majority. It has succeeded far beyond all others in those safeguards of equality of opportunity through education, public information, and the open channels of free speech and free press."[25]

Despite such successes as the above, Hoover goes on to note that the greatest troubles and failures of American government lie in the economic field and that the increased regulating function of the government is at once the greatest threat to, and the most potent force for the maintenance of, individualism. The growing complexities of industry and commerce require government regulation to prevent domination and unfair practices. The laissez faire of Adam Smith, then, has long since been abandoned; and Hoover sheds no tear for it. Two questions, however, must always be asked regarding governmental regulation: "Does this act safeguard an equality of opportunity? Does it maintain the initiative of our people"?[26] Easy questions to pose, but difficult ones to answer.

Yet, Hoover is once more optimistic, in terms of both the past and the future. The nation has made great progress in such areas as invention, production, distribution, standard of living, and education. Moral standards, too, he sees as having improved. And, like a good Puritan, the nation roots up and exposes wrongs. But whatever faults the nation has—and Hoover recognizes that there are some—a balance of perspective must be struck, for a "single crime does not mean a criminal society."[27]

VI *Whither Individualism?*

In the final chapter of *American Individualism*, Hoover once again emphasizes the uniqueness of individualism as it has flourished in America. He credits it with being the prime motivating force in the nation's development, picturing the American pioneer as "the epic expression of that individualism."[28] Nor are the days of the pioneer over, for Hoover sees more frontiers to conquer, among them, new continents of human welfare and new worlds of science. And again he warns of the destructive aspects of socialism as they relate to individualism. Perhaps, for the Old World, socialism "may have something to recommend it as an intellectual stop-look-and-listen sign,"[29] but not for America. "Salvation will not," he writes, "come to us out of the wreckage of individualism. What we need today is steady devotion to a better, brighter, broader individualism—and individualism that carries increasing responsibility and service to our fellows."[30]

With that clarion call forward, he goes on to warn against destructively critical minds that are incapable of nurturing constructive ideas; for destructive criticism can lead to revolution. And, as we have seen from the very beginning of *American Individualism*, Hoover has a consummate fear of revolution, which he sees as "no summer thunderstorm clearing the atmosphere," but as "a tornado leaving in its path the destroyed homes of millions with their dead women and children."[31] So strong is this fear that when he espouses such ideals as freedom of speech, we can feel a slight tinge of uneasiness in the tenacity with which he takes a position. When he writes that "there is no oratory so easy, no writing so trenchant and vivid as the phrase-making of criticism and malice—there is none so difficult as inspiration to construction,"[32] we are left with the question as to who defines criticism and inspiration.

Hoover is optimistic that in the long run right ideas will triumph, but he is not willing to leave it at that. It is too easy for men to succumb to wrong ideas and wrong social philosophies—indeed, the "declines of civilization have been born of wrong ideas. Most of the wars of the world, including the recent one, have been fought by the advocates of contrasting ideas of social philosophy."[33] Here, certainly, is the seed from which later springs Hoover's isolationist tendencies, at least regarding America's involvement in European political problems.

The task for America, therefore, is to understand clearly the nature of its individualism, to keep it inviolate by preserving and stimulating the initiative of people and by safeguarding the equality of opportunity. Thus will come "a social system as perfect as our generation merits and one that will be received in gratitude by our children."[34]

VII A Celebration and a Warning

American Individualism, rightly enough, is a simply expressed sermon. And, like a sermon, it both celebrates and warns. There are no deep philosophical thrusts into the nature of man or of society. Hoover is content to lay out as neatly as he can a pattern of life that will result in what he sees as an optimum society. True, the pattern is based on an ideal; but the impression is that it is done so almost in passing—as if Hoover the engineer and administrator is much more interested in the working of the system than in its sources. For, after all, he was a man whose primary goal in life had always been to make things work. This is not to deny the humanitarian feelings that certainly were a part of his makeup, but simply to put into perspective his actions and statements. The danger here is that the social machine as a unit may become more important than the effects of that machine upon individual people.[35]

American Individualism shows Hoover to be both liberal and conservative in his views of the development of American society—liberal in that he sees equality of opportunity as a vital component of that society and conservative in that he is wary lest too much experimentation might ruin a good thing. This dual aspect of his position gave him no real problems in writing *American Individualism*. As one reviewer said, "he has the mind that doubts and analyzes, but the will that constructs and believes."[36] His stance on American individualism as a standard of civilization and progress is unyielding. No matter that some might say that it was "Old World individualism that gave birth to the new American individualism, which in its new vigor and strength, became more acquisitive, more ruthless in the exploitation of virgin soil"[37]—Hoover remains steadfast in his view that American individualism is unique, that it sprang from the peculiar circumstances of the settlement and development of America.

Frederick Jackson Turner, whose own theories of the influence of the frontier in America's development have had such widespread impact on the study of American history, after having read *American Individualism,* wrote to Hoover that "it is the platform on which all genuine Americans can stand, a noble statement of the fruits of our past and the promise of our future."[38]

Others, too, wrote Hoover in praise of *American Individualism.* Mario S. Saija, of the Italian-American News Bureau, said that "it is not a message to the great American People only, but it should be also the exponent of American ideals for those other people, here and abroad, who do not understand America and its institutions."[39] A Russian scholar living in Paris offered to translate *American Individualism* into Russian because "I think, for the Russian brains, so shaken, so upset by the class spirit, it will be a good thing to read your vigorous plea for the intrinsic qualities and capacities of human nature."[40] Don Beltran Mathieu, Ambassador of Chile, who translated *American Individualism* into Spanish, wrote, "My purpose is to make it known to some of my friends and prominent people in Chile because in the confusion introduced by the revolutionary propaganda, and by the fantasies of idealists, whose theories are thought new and which, generally, are old, I believe it advisable to establish the real and true principles of government."[41] A bit less sanguine was the letter from Horace D. Taft of the Taft School: "I wish I were more optimistic. I see enough of the finest kind of human nature, plenty of good feeling and kindliness and plenty of idealism, but so many of these boys are surrounded by a kind of jazz life at home and they go into such a bath of it at college that it is hard for a man to keep his courage."[42]

While most of the responses to *American Individualism* were positive, others were of a negative turn. Hugo E. Walters, an avowed Communist, wrote to Hoover that he, Hoover, was caught by a will-o'-the wisp in his views of individualism, because only when the inheritance of private property is abolished can there be real equality of opportunity.[43] The *Weekly People* made the following points in a review:

He does not take a step before he becomes entangled in the meshes of his own argument. "Production," he says, "both of mind and hand rests upon impulses in each individual. These impulses are made of the varied forces of original instincts, motives, and acquired desires." But many of these instincts, etc., he tells us, are destructive and therefore "must be restrained through moral leadership and authority of the law and be eliminated, finally, by education." We see, then, that society— that is "agreements, organizations, institutions, masses or groups"— or. . .the "leaders" of such are those who in the last analysis modify or beat into shape the intelligence, character, courage and the divine spark of the human soul of the individual. Hence these are but the results of the action and reaction of outside influences.[44]

Whatever else it is, *American Individualism* is an attempt at a composite, reduced to essence, of many things Hoover tried to do in his own life—a codification of beliefs that he really acted upon. Moreover, we can hardly deny that, for the most part, he succeeded. For him, American individualism was no will-o'-the wisp, no obscure ideal lurking just beyond reach. His expression of it in the tightly knit little book that we have just examined may be stilted, trite on occasion, and perhaps even contradictory in places. The essential point, however, is that he felt his version of individualism to be so real and so cogent for America that he could, indeed, write it down for the rest of us to read and thus to gain valuable insight into our past heritage and our future hopes.

CHAPTER 4

A Tale Of Two Campaigns

HERBERT Hoover gave over 600 major addresses between 1919 and 1962—an impressive number under any circumstances, but even more so in light of Hoover's distaste for public speaking. For him, making a speech was a duty that had to be performed, and he was always glad when each performance of that duty was over.

Theodore G. Joslin, who served as secretary to President Hoover from 1931 through 1932, discusses Hoover's speech preparation in his very informative book titled *Hoover Off the Record* (1934):

Writing speeches was his hardest work. First, he would set down in longhand thoughts that came to him, lining and interlining until the most skilled compositor, if unacquainted with his hand, would have had difficulty in deciphering the words. Then a stenographer would make a typewritten copy. She had to know her business. At best his writing was none too legible. And he had a system of abbreviation all of his own. It included one peculiarity to which I never quite adapted myself. The adjective "the" was such a teeny word that it did not need three letters. He always wrote it "he," with the slightest curve at the top of the "h." That answered for the "t."

With the typewritten copy, always triple-spaced, back in his hands, he would go over it again and again, reconstructing, striking out some of the original ideas, bringing in new ones and rephrasing again and again.

Having put down on paper the thoughts he wished to convey, although with no regard to sequence and often as little to form, he would send the latest version to the printer for a dozen proofs. The process would be resumed after the proofs came back. Some of these proofs would be distributed among officials and friends for the dual purpose of getting their ideas and to make sure of accuracy.

I might say that scientific preciseness governed all his writing, once the effort approached final form. An engineer by training, he built his public utterances as he would drive a mine shaft or construct a bridge.

61

He would search his storehouse of words for those that would interpret his exact thought, testing each and every one for stress and strain, and then interlocking them with a fine network of minor words like the web of wires on a suspension bridge. Those that fell short of the necessary requirements he ruthlessly discarded, as he would a steel beam in which a flaw had been discovered. But the final result was the work of a craftsman. The principal criticism to make of his addresses is that each one was too correct in detail, too precise, for the casual listener or reader.[1]

Those speeches Hoover gave during his two presidential campaigns provide insight not only into the structural approaches he relied upon in his speeches, but also into his basic views of the problems facing America at the time and his strategies for solving them. The two groups of campaign speeches appear in *The New Day* (1928) and *Campaign Speeches of 1932* (1933), respectively.

I   *Greeting the New Day*

Hoover received formal notice of his nomination in 1928 from Senator George Moses, who had traveled from Washington, D.C., to the latter's Stanford, California, home. Sixty thousand persons gathered in the Stanford University stadium to hear Hoover's address of acceptance on August 11, 1928.

In this address, Hoover saw the problems of the future as problems of construction. The reconstruction necessitated by World War I was over: "New and gigantic forces have come into our national life. The Great War released ideas of government in conflict with our principles. We have grown to financial and physical power which compels us into a new setting among nations. Science has given us new tools and a thousand inventions."[2] Surely it was a time of construction, but Hoover cautioned that the nation must not succumb to the temptation to venture away from those principles upon which the republic was founded and upon which it has grown to greatness.

The picture Hoover presented of the United States was one in which constructive leadership and cooperation had released the energies of the people—moving the nation to the threshold of widened opportunity for all. Grinding poverty for all those willing to work was well on the way to being abolished, and soon the poorhouse would be only a memory. The American home, the sanctuary of American ideals and the source of the spiritual energy of the American people, had reached a new level of strength and quality. Still, America must be careful not to perceive economic advancement as an end in itself; and Hoover stated that ther must be a "constant regard for those human values that give dignity and nobility to life. Generosity of impulse, cultivation of mind, willingness to sacrifice, spaciousness of spirit—those are the qualities whereby America, growing bigger and richer and more powerful, may become America great and noble."[3]

In discussing government and business, Hoover pointed to the magnificent progress America had made as proof of the "fundamental correctness of our economic system. Our pre-eminent advance over nations in the last eight years has been due to distinctively American accomplishments."[4] These accomplishments he spoke of were not simply the result of vast natural resources, but derived from the basic character of the American people—the same character that gave birth to the individualism that Hoover wrote and talked about so much. Hoover showed, however, that he accepted the growing complexities of American economic life and the accompanying need for government and business to work together. The rules of such interaction were, for Hoover, quite simple: "It is the duty of government to avoid regulation as long as equal opportunity to all citizens is not invaded and public rights violated. Government should not engage in business competition with its citizens. . . . On the other hand, it is the duty of business to conduct itself so that government regulation or government competition is unnecessary."[5]

Coming together here once more is that interesting combination of the practical and the ideal that we can see so often in Hoover's career. He accepted without question the practical aspect of business; his career certainly reflects that acceptance. At the same time, however, he saw business as very much founded upon faith—faith in the integrity of businessmen. A very neat combination indeed. Still, he seems to have had some doubt as to the strength of this marriage of practicality and faith without the working of government to maintain that faith. To put it another way, business must have a high sense of moral responsibility; and government has the duty of seeing to it that business maintains that high sense of moral responsibility.

For his second campaign speech, Hoover returned to his birthplace—West Branch, Iowa—on August 21, 1928. A crowd of over 12,000, mostly farmers from Iowa and Illinois, jammed the tiny village and the huge tent in which Hoover spoke.

In reminiscing upon his boyhood in West Branch, Hoover saw it as a place that symbolized the great strides made by American agriculture since his days there. With these great strides that so effectively helped to raise America's standard of living, though, came greater possibilities for anxiety because of the increased effect of price fluctuations. Hoover gladly accepted both of these factors: "While we recognize and hold fast to what is permanent in the old-time conditions, we must accept what is inevitable in the changes that have taken place. It is fortunate indeed that the principles upon which our government was founded require no alteration to meet these changes."[6]

Hoover spoke to the farmers that day about farm relief, interior waterways, and a St. Lawrence seaway—all projects designed for the growth of American industry, agricultural and otherwise. But as he did so, he reminded them that the real basis of American democracy lay in equality of opportunity. "Here there are no limits to hope," he said, "no limits upon accomplishment; our obligation today is to maintain that equal opportunity for agriculture as well as for every other industry."[7]

Hoover's third speech was delivered in Newark, New Jersey, on September 17, 1928. He centered his remarks on the importance of stable employment as the foundation of the nation's economic progress and on the necessity for sound policies and vigorous cooperation by the government and business to insure such stability. He relegated labor to a lesser position in terms of its ability to aid in achieving full employment: "Labor in its collective efforts has contributed greatly to the maintenance of proper wages and to improved conditions of labor. But collective bargaining cannot overcome the forces that make for unemployment. I, for one, am willing to trust the proved ability of employees to take care of their rights if there is employment to be had."[8]

Enumerating a number of the policies followed by the Republican Party to reach full employment and to insure economic growth, Hoover justified the protective tariff, restrictions upon immigration, and measures to increase foreign trade.

Beyond these steps, he saw others as essential. The buying power of farmers, for example, needed to be increased so that it in turn would add to the security of employment in other industries. Industrial and commercial efficiency needed to be increased, because efficiency is the track upon which runs a train of consequences consisting of increased production, higher wages, lower prices, increased consumption in both domestic and foreign markets, increased demand for labor, and a higher standard of living. "The ancient bitter opposition to improved methods on the ancient theory that it more than temporarily deprives men of employment," he argued, "has no place in the gospel of American progess."[9]

Like so many other politicans and economists, Hoover pointed to the need for measures to mitigate the impact of the "boom-bust" characteristics of the business cycle. His suggested remedies include better organization of credit; statistical prediction regarding the demand for, and production of, industrial products; and the use of public construction during slack times.

Returning near the end of this speech to the question of employer-employee relations, Hoover reasserted the Republican position of support of free collective bargaining. From the tone of his comments, we might infer that Hoover would wish that there were no need for collective bargaining, that responsible cooperation between employer and employee would be enough to reduce or eliminate conflict. Such a situation would truly reflect the American ideal. He made a wishful leap toward this ideal when he said,

The large majority of both sides today willingly accept the fundamental principle that the highest possible wages are the road to increased consumption of goods and thereby to prosperity. Both accept the fundamental fact that greater efficiency, larger application of mechanical devices, and full personal effort are the road to cheaper costs, lower prices, and thus again to wider consumption and larger production of goods. Both discard the ancient contention that labor is an economic commodity. Both realize that labor is entitled to participation in the benefits of increased efficiency by increased wage, either directly or through the decrease in living costs. Both have joined in repelling socialism and other subversive movements.[10]

On October 6, 1928, at Elizabethtown, Tennessee, Hoover

spoke on the occasion of the one hundred forty-eighth anniver-
sary of the Battle of King's Mountain. As any good politician
would, he spent considerable time extolling the greatness of the
South and of southern pioneers. He also drew a parallel between
his own heritage and the South—his great-great-grandfather
having migrated west from Maryland. Admitting that he was a
candidate of a political party often opposed in Tennessee, he
hastened to add that "so closely welded in common interest are
the pressing issues of our nation today that it should be no longer
unusual for a citizen of any region to vote for a president who
represents the principles which correspond with his convictions."[11] And it wasn't, for Hoover carried the state of Tennessee
in the election.

Three halls were filled when Hoover spoke in Boston on
October 15, 1928—the Arena, where Hoover gave his speech;
Tremont Temple; and historical Mechanics' Hall. He made no
apologies for speaking bluntly on economic questions, particularly as they were affected by the tariff and foreign trade.

Recognizing that New England's prosperity had long been tied
to foreign trade, he did not spare the adjectives in praising the
New Englanders' commercial and industrial skills that over the
generations made them so successful in providing products for
both domestic and foreign markets. And from that point of
praise, he went on to show the broader implications of foreign
trade and to explain and justify the Republican policies in regard
to that trade—not too difficult a task, considering the number of
protected industries in New England. His major concern,
however, was to show that the various aspects of foreign trade
were not simply local issues. The pattern of economics had
become such that what touched one area eventually touched all
others.

Again, as in almost every other speech he made, Hoover closed
by moving beyond material things to celebrate spiritual things—
attributing to New England a great stimulus for the rest of the
nation: "New England taught us the ways of business. But you
gave us something far finer and more precious. You sent us men
and women on fire with the passion for truth and service."[12]

The only appearance that Hoover made in New York during
the 1928 campaign came on October 22, when he spoke in
Madison Square Garden. He focused his remarks not on the many
issues that had been discussed during the campaign, but on what

he referred to as more fundamental principles and ideals. The war, he pointed out, necessitated the regimentation of "our whole people temporarily into a socialistic state. However justified in time of war, if continued in peacetime it would destroy not only our American system but with it our progress and freedom as well."[13] The choice at the end of the war—not only in America, but in all the world—was whether such regimentation should continue. "We were," he said, "challenged with a peacetime choice between the American system of rugged individualism and a European philosophy of diametrically opposed doctrines—doctrines of paternalism and state socialism."[14]

Hoover saw nothing positive in the government's attempting to go into commerical business. Whenever it does, he said, "it immediately finds itself in a labyrinth, every alley of which leads to the destruction of self-government."[15] It had to decide whether leadership and direction were to come from appointment by political agencies or by election. And here Hoover fell back on his pragmatic principle that leadership in business must come through the sheer rise in ability and character. Bureaucracy, he felt, precluded the free atmosphere of competition necessary for the most able persons to reach leadership positions. Moreover, because the nation's legislative bodies cannot delegate their full authority to individuals or to commissions, when government goes into commercial business, "five hundred and thirty-one Senators and Congressmen become the actual board of directors of that business."[16] And the same situation occurs at the state level.

The growth of such bureaucracy was, of course, anathema to Hoover. Echoing his statements in *American Individualism,* he indicted bureaucracy as the poison that could destroy the very roots of liberalism and lead the nation not to more liberty, but to less liberty. "Liberalism," he remarked, "is a force truly of the spirit, a force proceeding from the deep realization that economic freedom cannot be sacrificed if political freedom is to be preserved."[17]

Walking once more that fine line between too much government interference and just enough government protection, Hoover went on to praise the flexibility of the American system and to say that his view and that of the Republican party should not be interpreted as "free-for-all and devil-take-the-hindmost," but as government regulation only when necessary to prevent abuses and to protect the rights of Americans, particularly the right of equality of opportunity. "My concept of America," he stated in conclusion, "is a land where men and women may walk in ordered freedom in the independent conduct of their occupations; where they may enjoy the advantages of wealth, not concentrated in the hands of the few but spread through the lives of all; where they build and safeguard their homes, and give to their children the fullest advantages and opportunities of American life; where every man shall be respected in the faith that his conscience and his heart direct him to follow."[18]

As the campaign wound down, Hoover, enroute to California to cast his own vote, made his last major address at the Coliseum in St. Louis on November 2, 1928. A counterpoint to his remarks in New York against the debilitating effects of too much government interference in business, the St. Louis speech dealt with what Hoover saw as the constructive side of government—a side made possible by the very uniqueness of the American system, based as it is "not only upon the ideal that all men are created equal and are equal before the law, but also upon the ideal that there shall be equal opportunity among men."[19]

Hoover described a tightly knit American system of new political, social, and economic ideas, no one part of which could be destroyed without undermining the whole. The success of the system proved its rightness, and "to adopt other social conceptions, such as federal or state government entry into commercial business in competition with its citizens, would undermine initiative and enterprise and destroy the very foundations of freedom and progress upon which the American system is builded."[20]

From that point, he moved deftly to the principles of the Republican party and the part they played in the nation's progress, showing once more how easily he could modulate between destructive government action and constructive government action. There were, in his mind, three potential areas in which the principles and impulses of the American system demanded constructive government action: (1) public works such as inland waterways, flood control, reclamation, highways, and public buildings; (2) education, public health, scientific research, public parks, conservation of national resources, agriculture, industry, and foreign commerce; and (3) cooperation among people toward useful social and economic ends. And he went on to discuss these areas in detail, closing with a glowing image of government as "more than administration; it is power for leadership and cooperation with the forces of business and cultural life in city, town, and countryside" and the Presidency as "more than executive responsibility. It is the inspiring symbol of all that is highest in America's purposes and ideals."[21]

An inspiring symbol himself in his victory, Hoover moved into the White House and, with a tremendous sense of responsibility, took over the duties of the presidency. Because he was considered by many to be the best qualified president in many years, he was expected to do great things. "Considering that the baffling Middle Westerner in the White House has started all this fresh stir of question and excitement," wrote Anne O'Hare McCormick in the *New York Times,* "and that the country is ready as it seldom has been for audacious leadership, the chance for coincidence between the man and the hour seems almost too good a historic opportunity to waste."[22] There may well have been the feeling in America that with Hoover's moving to the White House, a new sun was rising over Washington; but, as we have seen, it was in reality a sun setting.

II Losing the New Day

In accepting his party's nomination for a second term as president, Hoover's remarks were of a far different tone from those that he made in his 1928 acceptance speech. "The last three years," he said, "have been a time of unparalleled economic calamity. They have been years of greater suffering and hardship than any which have come to the American people since the aftermath of the Civil War."[23] Just what effect this period of economic and social crisis had on Hoover will probably never be fully known. That it had an effect is beyond question. Roy Peel and Thomas Donnelly, in their *The 1932 Campaign* (1935), saw considerable effect:

President Hoover was a changed man after he took the oath of office in 1928. The tremendously burdensome obligations of his office transformed him from a calm and collected candidate into a harassed and peevish executive. Furthermore, the public stereotype of the

Great Engineer and the Great Humanitarian faded from view as the powerful searchlight of publicity beat upon his past life. A number of debunking biographers, some of whom had been ready with the results of their inquiries during the campaign of 1928 but had had difficulty in finding publishers, now gained a hearing from a distressed and disillusioned people.[24]

However accurate the picture of Hoover presented by Peel and Donnelly, it is clear that in the 1932 campaign, he was on the defensive. The Republican strategy for the campaign was based on four points: (1) accept the fact of the Depression and blame it on Europe; (2) insist that under the Democrats the Depression would be far worse; (3) restore public confidence by making new promises; and (4) interpret the years 1930–1932 as a period when Hoover showed great resourcefulness in laying and executing plans to end the depression.

Hoover wasted no time in laying the blame for America's economic woes on the European doorstep. America may have been guilty of overexpansion and overspeculation,[25] but she would have been able to weather the resulting period of hardship had other factors not impinged. "We adopted policies in the Government," Hoover reminded the Republican convention and the nation, "which were fitting to the situation. Gradually the country began to right itself. Eighteen months ago there was a solid basis for hope that recovery was in sight."[26] Having thus established the point that his administration had been up to the challenge presented it, he went on to say,

Then there came to us a new calamity, a blow from abroad of such dangerous character as to strike at the very safety of the Republic. The countries of Europe proved unable to withstand the stress of the depression. The memories of the world had ignored the fact that the insidious diseases left by the Great War had not been cured. The skill and intelligence of millions in Europe had been blotted out by battle, disease, and starvation. Stupendous burdens of national debts had been built up. Poisoned springs of political instability lay in the treaties which closed the war. Fears and hates held armaments to double those before the war. Governments were fallaciously seeking to build back by enlarged borrowing, by subsidizing industry and employment with taxes that slowly sapped the savings upon which industry must be rejuvenated and commerce solidly built. Under these strains the financial systems of many foreign countries crashed one by one.[27]

Regardless of how Hoover perceived the strategy of his administration, it had incurred considerable displeasure across the nation. Perhaps people had been led to expect too much from the man who had peformed so well in America's efforts to feed much of Europe during and after World War I; or perhaps, as a number of historians and economists have said, Hoover did indeed misunderstand the full implications of the Depression and thus did not act directly to blunt its effects. Either way, for Hoover to run on his record was hardly a viable choice. Still, it was his only choice—and his campaign speeches of 1932 represent a valiant effort to restate the basic principles in which he so strongly believed.

On October 4, 1932, the beleaguered president returned to his home state of Iowa to speak in Des Moines. In what is considered one of his best speeches of the campaign, Hoover focused first on the steps that his administration had taken to protect the living, comfort, and safety of the American fireside. Had these steps not been taken, an infinitely greater harm would have befallen the nation. That was his justification for his actions—actions taken in a battle that "had to be fought in silence, without the cheers of the limelight or the encouragement of public support, because the very disclosure of the forces opposed to us would have undermined the courage of the weak and induced panic in the timid, which would have destroyed the very basis of success."[28]

The image, then, that Hoover presented of himself in this speech was that of the isolated and lonely executive carrying on the fight for the nation's survival amid "hideous misrepresentation and unjustified complaint" and "little public evidence of the dangers and enormous risks from which a great national victory has been achieved."[29]

Was he playing for sympathy? Possibly. But the above image, in one sense at least, fits Hoover better than perhaps he himself knew. He was not, as we have seen, one who would back away from a challenge. Yet, at the same time, he was one who functioned best when he was free to make his own decisions and to base action upon them. It is not strange, then, that he should have envisaged himself as a kind of knight errant on a quest to slay the dragon of depression and thus keep secure American principles and ideals.

Much of the Des Moines speech, of course, dealt with agricultural policies. In Cleveland, on October 15, he shifted his emphasis to employment problems and to defending the Hawley-Smoot tariff bill, which he hoped would reduce the difference in the cost of production at home and abroad. With regard to the latter, the Democrats, to Hoover's way of thinking, had been making "amazing" statements as to the debilitating effects it was having on foreign trade. His response to such criticism was simple and direct:

Do you want to compete with laborers whose wages in their own money are only sufficient to buy from one eighth to one third of the amount of bread and butter which you can buy at the present rates of wages? That is a plain question. It does not require a great deal of ingenious argument to support its correct answer. It is true we have the most gigantic market in the world today, surrounded by nations clamoring to get in. But it has been my belief—and it is still my belief—that we should protect this market for our own labor; not surrender it to the labor of foreign countries as the Democratic Party proposes to do.[30]

Whatever his theme or whoever his audience, Hoover never failed in his speeches to return to those spiritual guide-ons that he felt to be so essential a part of the American makeup and that he was sure would lead the nation out of the chaos of depression. He closed his Cleveland speech on that note:

We have been fighting not only as an administration but as a people, to relieve distress, to repel impending catastrophes, to restore the functioning of our economic life. This economic system has but one end to serve. That end is not the making of money. It is to create security in the millions of homes of our country, to produce increasing comfort, to open wider the windows of hope, to increase the moral and spiritual stature of our people, to give opportunity for that understanding upon which national ideals and national character may be more and more strengthened.

In securing these ends the first necessity is to preserve those precious heritages and principles which have come down to us forged in the fires of long generations of Americans. Principles and institutions which, while they have the imperfections of humanity, yet represent the highest expressions of human attainment in thousands of years.[31]

And so it went. To Detroit, where he attempted to correct a few of the many Democratic statements that he saw as misstatements—documenting his efforts at reducing government expenditures with a barrage of dollar figures that surely must have left the audience, if not totally lost, at least considerably confused. To Indianapolis, where he contrasted his policies with those proposed by Franklin Roosevelt and decried the slurs he felt were being uttered against not only his policies, but his character. To New York City, where he pictured the campaign as going beyond a contest between two men or two parties to a contest between two philosophies of government—one that, in the name of efficiency, would destroy the freedoms of the American system against one that would continue to build its programs within a framework that would safeguard those freedoms. To St. Louis, where he hotly denied the Democratic accusation that the Republican party was responsible for "this world-wide catastrophe" and where he attempted to educate his audience to the "evasions and misleading character of the campaign of the Democratic Party."[32] To St. Paul, where he paid special tribute to the American woman, who played such a heroic role in the nation's development and who "frequently take a longer view of American life than do a great many men."[33] To Salt Lake City, where, expressing relief and stimulation from being back in the West, he placed his strongest emphasis on what he saw as an even greater problem than the economic depression—the problem of the prevention of future wars:

I see in wars the loss of the glorious young manhood of the world who, but for war's slaughter, would lead the bright columns of human hope and human idealism and human progress to levels far above the past. I see wars in terms of women, widowed or unwed, with fond hopes blasted, of homes and children. I see war's most lamentable casualties in homes wrecked and in homes that never even had their chance of being. I see wars in terms of children born into lives foredoomed to ignorance and the toil that dwarfs both mind and spirit. I see war's fatal poison subtly invading the moral ideals of the people, bringing grossness and cynicism where should grow the fine flower of idealism. The world has seen enough of a post-war peace that is not peace, but rather smoulders on in racial hatreds.[34]

Hoover must have been physically and emotionally drained when he arrived at Elko, Nevada, on November 7 for his last speech of the campaign. He described the completed campaign as one of "education in great domestic and international problems which have arisen out of the events of the last fifteen years."[35] And he once again appealed to the women voters, with whom "lies largely the guardianship of the fundamental ideals, because concentrated in their lives and their responsibilities is a solicitude for the preservation of the home and the inspiration for the future of our children."[36] The campaign was over, and so too was Herbert Hoover's political career.

The speeches of Herbert Hoover, whatever their occasion, read very much alike. Reflecting the same kind of tight organization that Hoover utilized in his engineering career, they are direct, concrete, and instructional. He saw every speaking occasion as an opportunity to educate his audience, and virtually every speech was constructed with that idea in mind. In his efforts to make the abstract concrete, Hoover disdained name calling, emotional appeals, and charged expressions. As Howard Runkel, in a study of Hoover's speeches, says, "most of Hoover's appeals are indirect. This lack of boldness in *pathos* does not signify a dearth of appeals, for the speeches are replete with emotional drive. In Hoover's speeches, however, this drive is distinctly subordinated to the argumentative development—the element of *logos*."[37]

The organizational pattern of Hoover's speeches moves from an identification and analysis of the problem in question, through a discussion of pertinent solutions, to a choice of the most practical solution. Runkel describes Hoover's ideas in his speeches as revealing "that his issues are lasting issues and that his demonstrative utterances evolve out of and get their fundamental material from practical, matter-of-fact human affairs. He never engages in forensic discourses on transitory themes. . . . His ideas were exclusively those which 'make a difference' in human affairs."[38]

Even a cursory examination of Hoover's speeches reveals what might be expected, given everything that is known about the man and his career—namely, a heavy style lacking variety and rhythm, but a content marked by an integrity of purpose and principles.

CHAPTER 5

Liberty and Liberalism

THE twelve years that followed the publication of Hoover's *American Individualism* (1922) saw him reach the pinnacle of his public career, as he moved from Secretary of Commerce to President of the United States. His political star, however, as we have seen, fell even more abruptly than it rose. At sixty years of age Herbert Hoover, for the first time since his graduation from Stanford, was unemployed—a strange and uncomfortable position for a man of his energy and drive and penchant for service. Moreover, as Eugene Lyons relates, "Hoover left the White House in a time of sorrow and anguish. The fates, with some hefty mortal help, had contrived to bring the depression to its nadir precisely at the moment of his departure. Why shouldn't the cheerful newcomers, dangling their bag of tricks, show contempt for his trivial person?"[1]

Because Lyons in his biography is somewhat less than objective in his praise of Hoover's accomplishments as a politician and statesman, we are prone to discount some of what he says. Yet, he is essentially correct in his estimation of the regard in which Hoover was held when he left office, not only by the "cheerful newcomers," but also by the nation at large. The reality of the Depression, coupled with the smear campaign against him, was indeed Hoover's political undoing. Few presidents have left office under so dark a cloud.

For almost two years, Hoover, at least publicly, held his silence with regard to the New Deal and its "bag of tricks." In the spring of 1935, however, Hoover made a number of public statements that made many wonder whether he was laying the groundwork for another run for the presidency in 1936. In a speech to the Republican assembly in Sacramento, California, on March 22, he charged the Republican party with the responsibility of furnishing the rallying point for the American people as they faced the

choice of "maintaining and perfecting our system of orderly
individual liberty under constitutionally conducted government,
or of rejecting it in favor of the newly created system of
regimentation and bureaucratic domination in which men and
women are not masters of government but are the pawns or
dependents of a centralized and potentially self-perpetuating
government."[2] But, even though he was still titular head of his
party, there was little chance for Hoover to win the Republican
nomination. As Harry Brown commented in the *Salt Lake
Tribune,* "the fact is that every time Hoover speaks, cold shivers
run up and down the spine of Republicans who have begun to
take heart, and who are beginning to believe they may have a
chance in the 1936 election."[3]

Hoover also had been working on another book—one that
would not only enlarge upon his statements in *American
Individualism,* but one that would also reaffirm in his own mind
and in the minds of his readers the enduring strengths of the
American system. That book was *The Challenge to Liberty*
(1934).

I   *Once More into the Breach*

If Hoover thought that the ideal of Liberty was under siege in
1922 when he wrote *American Individualism,* he was sure in
1934 that it was under direct attack. And once more he was
ready to spring to its defense. Much had occurred in that twelve-
year span to make many wonder whether free institutions could
survive the powerful social forces unleashed by World War I and
by the rapid advancement of industrial technology. Hoover
feared that, in an effort to control such forces and such advances,
nations would destroy "those fundamental human liberties which
have been the foundation and the inspiration of progress since
the Middle Ages."[4]

His first step in *The Challenge to Liberty* is to define liberty. It
is, he says, "a thing of the spirit—to be free to worship, to think,
to hold opinions, and to speak without fear—free to challenge
wrong and oppression with surety of justice."[5] Having established this spiritual and idealistic base, he postulates that such
freedoms as the above cannot exist unless there are also
economic freedoms. Again we have the wedding of the ideal and

the practical. Hoover, it seems, was never able for very long to conceive of an ideal in anything other than an economic context. Material and moral achievements are seen as springing from the same spiritual and intellectual source.

From the concept of liberty comes that mode of thought called liberalism, which holds that the former is "an endowment from the Creator of every individual man and woman upon which no power, whether economic or political, can encroach, and that not even the government may deny."[6] The liberal of more recent times might find such a view of liberalism a bit too narrow, but Hoover had no such problem. He had not the least doubt that, once the constructive instincts and aspirations of man are released, society will move inevitably forward toward its goal of human betterment.

This Jeffersonian echo makes Hoover vulnerable to the charge of naiveté from those who see the necessity for man's instincts and aspirations to be controlled. Such a charge, however, is not entirely warranted, because Hoover was well aware that there was still a long way for humanity to travel on the road to social and economic perfection. "I would indeed be glad," he writes, "to find a short cut to end the immensities of human problems. I have no word of criticism but rather great sympathy with those who honestly search human experience and human thought for some easy way out, where human selfishness has no opportunities, where freedom requires no safeguards, where justice requires no striving, where bread comes without contention and with little sweat."[7]

While the path of liberty may be long and hard, it must not, in Hoover's mind, be rejected for the many alternate paths suggested by political and economic dreamers—paths that would only "lead either to the swamps of primitive greed or to political tyranny."[8] Fascism, communism, socialism—all may sing their hypnotic songs of promise and shout their Utopian slogans and phrases, but all will in the end sacrifice humanity in the name of expediency.

Thus, just as he was in *American Individualism,* Hoover is here concerned with the wave of revolutions sweeping the world, not in outright civil war so much as in the insidious chipping away at liberal institutions from within, the subtle breaking down of confidence in existing forms of government, and the ultimate imposition of a whole new complex of ideas and ideals upon a nation. Obviously, Hoover felt that such a revolution was threatening America itself.

The purpose of *The Challenge to Liberty*, then, is

to survey briefly the movement of revolution through the world since the Great War, and the method of overthrow of Liberalism; to recall our American heritage, the growth of our Liberty, the forces in human nature and human behavior which govern economic life, the restraints and ideals of the system of ordered Liberty, the achievements of the American System; to analyze from an American point of view the alternate systems of society; to examine our own abuses of Liberty; to review the purposes of American life; to consider constructively, not a detailed program, but the method through which alone we can solve national problems.[9]

II   *The Utility and Ideals of Liberty*

In *American Individualism* Hoover makes clear that he is discussing a unique kind of individualism—American individualism. In *The Challenge to Liberty* he makes the same point with the same clarity when he speaks of American liberalism. "I do not speak," he says, "of British Liberalism or French Liberalism. I do not speak of the Liberalism of the eighteenth century or the early Victorians. I speak of American Liberalism."[10] He does not see liberty nor liberalism as beginning in America, but he does see America as the only nation in which the whole social philosophy of liberty was set into the structure of government. Liberty, then, is rooted deep in the soil of America and is an accepted part of the lives of Americans—and liberalism is "a living creed, advancing to meet the problems of our particular world."[11]

The dynamic quality of American liberalism, while responsible for the growth and development of America, also gives rise to problems resulting from that growth. Constant reform, therefore, is necessary—and Hoover accepts that necessity. What he does not accept is any adjustment that will militate against the basic individual rights implicit in the American concept of liberty. And, though he does not mention it specifically, here is where he sees the New Deal as a threat. Accepting without equivocation the Natural Rights theory, Hoover emphasizes that

not even government—which itself derives from the people—
has the right to trespass upon the basic liberties.

Echoing his argument of *American Individualism,* Hoover
stresses the necessity for civilization to motivate the individual to
action and achievement. Prerequisite to such motivation is, of
course, an understanding of human nature, which Hoover views
as a duality of evil and selfish instincts and impulses on the one
hand and altruistic instincts and impulses on the other. The
former drive man to hatred, greed, and destruction, while the
latter inspire him to love, justice and service.

Such a clearcut division of instincts and impulses might lead us
to the conclusion that Hoover saw man not as a social creature,
but as simply an equation of those instincts and impulses—
certainly not a liberal view by today's definition. He says,
however, that "these instincts and qualities vary in proportion in
every individual and their proportions are modified by intelligence, ability, and physical vigor. They are further modified by
education, by moral and spiritual training, by the vast fund of
human experience, and the vast plant and equipment of
civilization which we pass on with increments to each succeeding
generation."[12] Having made the point that man, at least to a
degree, is a social creature, Hoover quickly reminds us that there
"can be no human thought, no impulse to action, which does not
arise from the individual."[13]

Here, in a sense, is the answer to the problem posed by
Whitman in "Democratic Vistas." Man is at once an individual
and a part of the mass. Each individual is a potential source of
material and spiritual progress, yet there exist immutable
economic laws that stem from the mass—such laws being "the
deduction from human experience of the average response of
these varied selfish or altruistic raw materials of the human
animal when applied in the mass."[14] Virtually every action of
Hoover's life reflects this view, and his response to the "amateur
sociologists [the New Dealers] who are misleading this nation" is
that no "economic equality can survive the working of biological
inequality."[15]

The American economic system that has developed out of all
this is one based on property, production, and profit, with
rewards to those who, to repeat a phrase, can stand up to the
"emery wheel of competition." Competition is the key in this
matrix, for Hoover strongly believes that neither leadership nor

creativity comes from birth, but only from the "sifting test of competition among free men and women."[16] No better illustration of this can be had, perhaps, than a comment Hoover's good friend Hugh Gibson made in a letter to Lewis Einstein, the American minister to Prague, concerning Hoover's handling of subordinates: "Hoover's method was to size a man up roughly, throw him into a position and dump responsibility on him. If the man stood up under the responsibility. . .he eventually fitted into his own place, either somewhat lower than where he started or as much higher as his ability took him. If the responsibility broke his back, out he went, because there was no time for coddling the incompetent."[17]

Hoover knew well enough that defending the American system solely on economic and/or political terms would not lend to it the sanctity demanded by the emotions of a nation. With utility, there must be ideals. Taking an a priori stance, Hoover points to the ideals of truth and justice and to spiritual yearnings within men and women. But these are never wholly realized; indeed, total realization of them is an impossibility. Nevertheless, they stand as beacons of guidance—as proof that the primary concern of America is not to grow rich economically, but to encourage the spiritual health and growth of men and women. Naive? Perhaps. But it is part of the circular construct that Hoover gives to liberty and liberalism.

He completes the circle by returning once again to the idea of equality of opportunity, for humane as our system may be, it cannot long survive without economic freedom.

III   Strengths of the American System

Benito Mussolini may have predicted the demise of the liberal faith in 1934, but Hoover would not believe that the temples of liberalism were deserted. As an answer to Mussolini and those in America who, too, were urging a turning away from liberal ideals, Hoover points to the accomplishments that America has made with liberty and liberalism as guideposts. Recalling his many ventures in foreign lands, he sees no country that can compare with America in terms of kindliness, neighborliness, individual responsibility, prosperity, freedom of spirit, equal opportunity, and the like, and proceeds to praise American accomplishments lavishly—so much so that we are left with the impression that Americans are the most humane of all people and that America is indeed a Utopian dream come true.

Hoover's point in celebrating the American system is obviously not so much to answer Mussolini as it is to warn his countrymen of dangers closer to home than Italian fascism—namely, Roosevelt's New Dealism. Roosevelt was calling for a reappraisal of values. He said in 1932 that America was steering a course toward economic oligarchy, that at the end of another century all American business would be controlled by no more than a dozen corporations. Government had the obligation to step into the situation to insure the salvation of our economic structures. Hoover would not disagree with the basic premise that an economic oligarchy would be disastrous. He said so many times himself. But he would disagree with Roosevelt's methods of solution. Hoover could not bring himself to believe that the American system was not so inherently strong and just that it would not somehow weather this storm as it had those of the past—without the heavy hand of government interference.

In the process of his celebration, Hoover is selective in those aspects of the American system that he reviews. He declines, for example, to mention anything about racial discrimination in the South of that period; and he neatly sidesteps the basic causes of the depression, which he calls a "transitory paralysis," stemming from world-wide excesses. And he implies that had he remained in office, the depression would have been beaten without strikes and social upheaval.

The problems facing America, he believes, are not the result of any real weakness in the system. They are simply the upshot of the confusion caused by efforts to find answers to the problems. Moreover, he is optimistic that the present difficulties "do not justify the assumption that a system of life builded on such sacrifice over a century and a half with such a record of achievement should be discarded or crippled, or that the philosophy of Liberty is all wrong, or even that we must sacrifice some of our liberties."[18] America, to Hoover, was one of the last bastions of freedom, and the battle lines must be drawn here or they may well be drawn nowhere.

In his discussion of some of the alternative social and economic philosophies that were being offered as replacements for the American system, Hoover refers to earlier systems that, like these new alternatives, saw men as subservient to the state but quickly dismisses them as having no significance to the present, unless it be simply as laboratory records. We are again left with the impression that Hoover conceived of the American system not as part of a vast evolutionary process spanning many centuries, but as something that sprang full blown on the American continent, without antecedents of any kind. Certainly a romantic notion, but one that fit well with the idea so often prevalent in American history that America somehow was to stand before the world as an unadulterated, pristine example of liberty and liberalism.

By stating that there is little in the way of exposition of the philosophy and structure of this American system, Hoover justifies his own efforts at providing some. His first objective is "to clear some underbrush"—to emphasize the difference between the laissez-faire economic theory of the French Physiocrats of the eighteenth century and Adam Smith and the Hoover version of American individualism. Hoover made a number of efforts, both in writing and in public address, to divorce the two. He resents "the charge that every wickedness in high place is because of our devotion to laissez-faire."[19] The American system, he emphasizes, is not one of "let do" or "go as you please."

The first alternative to the American system that Hoover discusses is socialism, which has, he says, as its disguised or open objective equality in income, wages, or economic rewards and, therefore, stands at the opposite pole from American liberalism. For the "tenet of equality in true Liberalism is a tenet of equality in birth, equality before the law, and equality of opportunity as distinguished from equality of reward for services. True Liberalism insists that to equalize rewards and possession of material things robs the individual of free imagination, inventiveness, risk, adventure, and individual attainment, development of personality, and independence from a monotony that would sentence the soul to imprisonment."[20] In this comment we see once more Hoover's idea of the basic relationship between the material and the spiritual—or simply that the "emery wheel of competition" is good for the soul.

In light of the present problems of the United States Postal Service, one comment on the efficiency of socialism is not only humorous, but apropos: "One thing is a certainty: that if all industry, through the inescapable play of political and bureaucratic action, were reduced to the efficiency of the post office, we should fail within a few years to produce sufficient to feed, clothe, and care for our people."[21]

But Hoover sees a far more cogent threat from socialism than mere inefficiency, and that is the threat to democratic institutions. In his view, if socialism would have a chance at success, it must merge all the powers of government under despotic control. When such is attempted, the resulting demoralization of the economic system may well cause a counter movement toward fascism. Particularly in America, where there is a strong economic middle class, would this be a very real danger.

Hoover gives short shrift to communism, which he says is merely the imposition of socialism by violence. He holds Russia up as the classic example of the failure of communism. Hindsight shows that he was a bit premature in his judgment of the Soviet Union. He lumps socialism and communism together under one biting indictment: "Freedom of men's minds is more precious to the future of humanity than even the jam on their bread—which neither Socialism nor Communism will produce."[22]

Fascism in Italy and Nazism in Germany provided Hoover with two examples of what results from the fear of socialism or communism. In both cases, dictatorships arose from economic dislocation caused by the war and exacerbated by Socialist and Communist activities. In both cases, democracy was repudiated as a myth and authority was embraced as a panacea for all social and economic ills.

IV *The Spiral of Governmental Interference*

In the sixth and seventh chapters of *The Challenge to Liberty,* Hoover treats the regimentation theory of economics and government and its impact upon American liberalism, pointing to actions of the Roosevelt administration as examples of this theory put into practice. Listing a number of powers that Congress delegated to the office of the president for the purpose of bringing economic recovery to the nation, he describes the snowball effect that results from the use of those powers:

Powers once delegated are bound to be used, for one step drives to another. Moreover, some group somewhere gains benefits or privilege by the use of every power. Once a power is granted, therefore, groups begin to exert the pressure necessary to force its use. Once used, a vested interest is created which thereafter opposes any relaxation and thereby makes for permanence. But beyond this, many steps once taken set economic forces in motion which cannot be retrieved.[23]

Hoover decries the already considerable inroads that regimentation has made into industry, commerce, and agriculture. The large number of trade groups and advisory boards set up to regulate about ninety percent of the nation's business outside of farming (Hoover's estimate) will replace the essential elements of cooperation—free will and consent—with at best "coercive cooperation." The fixing of minimum prices and the restriction of output has the same effect as would the abolition of the anti-trust acts; and such a condition will result, says Hoover, in the control of business by large corporations. Smaller competitors, then, will be sacrificed as a result of this "most stupendous invasion of the whole spirit of Liberty that the nation has witnessed since the days of Colonial America."[24]

The case is the same with the farmer, whom Hoover sees as "the most tragic figure in our present situation."[25] Inflation, boom, mechanization, breakdown of foreign markets, and drought worked great hardship on the American farmer from World War I into the 1930s. The New Deal efforts at stabilizing production and prices served for Hoover as one more profound example of the inherent tendency of bureaucracy to enlarge its powers and to move further away from the practical aspects of human nature and economic experience until, ultimately, coercion and dictation will have replaced free competition in the economic arena and men will indeed be the pawns of the state.

As we might expect, Hoover lashes out at the Tennessee Valley Authority as an instance of deliberate governmental entrance into business in competition with the private sector. Such a move was, in Hoover's lexicon, socialism. And the departure from the gold standard by the United States was a departure from liberty. Refusing to accept the New Deal's stated objective of reducing unbearable debt by currency devaluation, Hoover describes such a move in *The Challenge to Liberty* as an unfair blow to honest creditors and thrifty savers.

Hoover admits that, at the time of the writing of *The Challenge to Liberty*, it was unclear just how far regimentation policies were to be extended in the banking and currency areas, but he is adamant that unless such policies are severely limited, the wounds of liberty will be many. Once more, the problem is how we choose to define liberty. Hoover certainly had his own unequivocal definition, but that definition was fairly limited — ironically, almost too abstract. With regard to the devaluation policy of the New Deal, there is little question that the debtors saw no erosion of liberty in that policy. On the contrary, they no doubt saw it as a practical effort at softening the effects of the Depression. To be sure, creditors would take another stance. But that is precisely the point: no government can be based on a concept so fixed, so inflexible that it cannot adjust to events. To take the position that events must adjust to a concept may well be construed as naive.

Hoover did recognize that the American system was not perfect and that the Depression brought a number of imperfections into focus. The programs and policies that he tried to implement in his own administration attest to that recognition. And, as he says in *The Challenge to Liberty*, "all reform entails some degree of experiment. I have no fear of experiments which take account of experience, do not remake the errors of history, and do not set out to experiment with the principles of Liberty."[26]

In the area of relief, for example, Hoover delineates a clearcut sequence of responsibility that is inherent in the American system. Starting from the premise that no American willing to work should go hungry, Hoover says that first is "the obligation of the individual to his neighbors, then of institutions, then of local communities, and then of the State governments."[27] Only if these fail should the federal government take action. And should the federal government have to act, Hoover does not object to indirect relief through public works or to direct relief should it come to that. His optimistic view, however, is that voluntary associative activities, which come naturally to free men, will be sufficient, and that the federal government should seldom, if ever, have to resort to the kind of planning and directing advocated by the New Deal.

Reiterating that the first step in regimentation or in national planning is an obvious concentration of political and economic power in the executive branch of government, Hoover cautions that it is not enough simply to say let the government do it, for it is not the government that does it. Rather it is the various

bureaus and agencies, made up of human beings with considerable powers, that do it—the bureaucracy, marked by "three
implacable spirits: self-perpetuation, expansion, and an incessant
demand for more power."[28] These spirits lead sequentially to
impatience with human faults, arrogance, and tyranny.

Hoover rejects regimentation as a vicious spiral of governmental interference with, and control of, those aspects of life
that have, under American liberalism, been reserved to the
individual. Though in the beginning, such interference may be
exerted in the name of corrective measures, it will ultimately
"stifle the very impulses to progress" and "drive a wedge
through the heart of a whole nation."[29] He is convinced that
government impingement upon business, agriculture, and social
welfare would be repulsive to the human instincts of millions of
people. "Civilization has advanced," Hoover says, "only
whenever and wherever the critical faculty in the people at
large has been free, alive and unpolluted. It slumps whenever
this is intimidated or suppressed. That is the most certain lesson
of history."[30]

V Dynamics of the American System

Having catalogued the various threats to liberty and liberalism
posed by regimentation in the guise of the New Deal, Hoover
returns once again to the constructive methods and dynamics of
the American system. A rejection of regimentation, fascism,
socialism, or communism does not mean that America must live
with the abuses that mark liberty. "The real alternative," he
maintains, "is to regenerate our system of Liberty."[31] The first
step in this regeneration is to identify the real abuses, the real
problems.

In laying out what he deems to be these real abuses and real
problems facing America, Hoover, in his usual optimistic fashion,
tends to play down their basic significance. He says, for instance,
that to view problems in the mass makes for a far more
forbidding picture than to break them down into their parts—to
view them factually and not emotionally. The difficulty here is
that, while it may be possible for one person to analyze
objectively the problems facing a nation, it is virtually impossible
for even a small part of the mass to do so. Surely, from his
knowledge of, and experience in, history, Hoover was aware of

that. But even if he was, his optimism remains unclouded in *The Challenge to Liberty*.

His first point is that because America's problems of the time are seen against a backdrop of depression, causes are confused with effects and the superficial confused with the fundamental—with the result that the tendency of many is to perceive an irreconcilable conflict between liberty and the modern industrial age. Hoover will not concede to such a perception. He sees a distinct difference between the permanent characteristics of the American system and the peculiar circumstances of a given time that result in temporal problems. Thus, "experiment must be based upon the tenets of Liberty and experience and not blind trial and error practiced upon Liberty itself."[32]

Herein lies one of the primary differences between Hoover and Roosevelt: Hoover wanted to be as sure as possible that whatever experiment was tried would work; Roosevelt, on the other hand, was willing to keep trying one thing after another until he found something that worked. Ironically, each accused the other of leading the nation into chaos—Roosevelt, because he felt Hoover didn't do enough; and Hoover, because he felt Roosevelt was destroying the foundations upon which Liberty was based.

Hoover, moreover, argues in *The Challenge to Liberty* that the last frontiers of economic development in America have not been reached, that we are not relegated simply to administering what has already been achieved in the way of industry and resources. Were he to have accepted such an assumption, he would, of course, have been repudiating his own concept of the dynamic forces of the American system—forces which lie deep below the surface and which are released only when men and women are free from repression and interference. The geographic frontier may be closed, but there remain for Hoover "vast continents. . .of thought, of research, of discovery, of industry, of human relations, potentially more prolific of human comfort and happiness than even the 'Boundless West.' "[33]

It is not the basic tenets of the American system, according to Hoover, that give rise to the abuses of liberty, but individual men. Logic, then, dictates, that men, not institutions—such as the economic system—should be punished for betrayals of public trust. Or, as he put it with a bit more drama, "we do not need to burn down the house to kill the rats."[34]

To Hoover, the best "rat trap," as we might expect, is competition—which, though it on occasion needs regulation, is "the most effective and dependable check upon rapacity and a preventive of economic domination and tyranny."[35] He accepts the idea of, and the necessity for, regulation; but he does so only with the greatest caution. Admittedly, the lines between liberty and economic oppression are not always clear; however, it is possible to discover those lines. And, once they are discovered and actions are indicated, those actions must be kept within the methods and principles of the American system. Government must be an umpire, not a director; for if it cannot be the former, how can it hope to be the latter?

VI *Depression and Recovery*

The last questions Hoover addresses himself to in *The Challenge to LIberty* are whether the Depression was a product of the economic system of liberty and whether that system can furnish recovery from it. In one sense, Hoover has been dealing with both of these questions throughout the book, and we can be fairly certain what his answers will be: no to the first and yes to the second.

Hoover's first basic point is that the American system is one that is designed for peace and that, while there were other factors contributing to the Depression, its depth and violence were enormously increased by the war and its aftermaths of inflation. His second point is that the depth of the Depression had been passed in the summer of 1932, as the "lifting effect of domestic and world measures and the natural forces of recovery became evident in every branch of national life."[36] Such progress was interrupted in America, however, by the election and subsequent changes of national policies. Nevertheless, Hoover reminds us, the tide was turned during his administration, and it was done so within the accepted tenets of liberty.

Military or trade wars, unbalanced budgets and accompanying inflation, unstable currencies, and boom-depression cycles—these are the major causes of economic instability. And man, because he is optimistic, speculates upon his hopes—making him subject to mass emotions, both in the direction of having his hopes realized and in the direction of fear at having them dashed. The challenge, from Hoover's perspective, is to fashion a system that will serve to temper optimism and allay fear as first steps in combating the causes of economic instability.

A major hope of both the individual and government lies in the areas of greater individual security and higher standards of living. The problem, as envisaged by Hoover, is the abolition of poverty among those who have the will to work without creating or encouraging a group of loafers. Again, he sees the possibility of solving the problem without destroying liberty.

At the root of the problem of individual security is the question of the distribution of national wealth and income. In viewing this question, Hoover discounts its significance somewhat: "But we may point out that with the diffusion of income in normal times under our system among 25,000,000 American families, it cannot be justly claimed that more than a fringe of a few hundred thousand receive more than they deserve for the service they give the community and that there are not more than a few million on the other fringe who conscientiously work and strive and do not receive that to which they are justly entitled. In between lies the vast majority of our people."[37]

Hoover has been accused of never acknowledging the weak purchasing power of the American people in contrast with the nation's powerful forces of production. Richard Hofstadter, in *The American Political Tradition* (1948), takes issue with Hoover's denial that there was any serious maldistribution of wealth in the United States:

The Brookings Institution study, *America's Capacity to Consume*, which appeared in the same year as *The Challenge to Liberty*, showed that the nation's 631,000 richest families had a total income considerably larger than the total income of 16,000,000 families at the bottom of the economic scale. From the standpoint of purchasing power, these 16,000,000 families, the Brookings economist concluded, had incomes too small even to purchase "basic necessities." Such was the potential market at home during the years when Secretary Hoover had been working so hard to expand American markets abroad.[38]

Regardless of Hoover's accuracy in his estimation of the distribution of wealth in America, he makes it clear that the undue amassing and concentration of wealth needs to be curbed. Such curbing, however, must be done slowly, "for violent action distributes more poverty than wealth."[39]

Hoover closes *The Challenge to Liberty* by restating the challenges and threats he sees facing liberty and liberalism and by extolling the strengths and virtues of those concepts. He has no doubt that they will, in the end, triumph: "In the methods of Liberty there is a vast constructive program before us. If we maintain its dynamic forces of life, if we strive for peace, if our economic system be cleared so far as humanly possible of abuse, if we develop the stability which is obviously attainable, if we advance personal security, then with vigilance in our moral and social responsibilities, the other many problems of the times will find their solutions."[40]

VII *Spiritual and Material Reconciliation*

In *The Challenge to Liberty*, then, Hoover makes a strong argument for what he sees as the unique American concepts of liberty and liberalism, which essentially are a single concept. He refuses to compromise his belief in the validity of this concept. The war and the vengeful peace following it, the encouragement of inflation to postpone war debts, the speculation that accompanies inflation—these factors, along with scientific advances and labor-saving devices, may cause problems of dislocation and depression; but such problems are not insoluble and do not mark the end of liberty and liberalism as viable bases for a nation, America in particular. The unbridled zeal of wild-eyed revolutionaries may, in the beginning, be sincerely motivated; but it all too quickly can lead to a greater and greater circumscription of liberty, even to dictatorship. The masses are told that it is necessary to surrender liberty in order to save it, that ultimately any surrendered freedoms will be returned fourfold. Hoover brands this the Big Lie. Once liberty is compromised, it can never be redeemed. Throughout the book, therefore, runs the warning that to sacrifice those aspects of liberty that have been developed over many years of travail in a frenzied effort to solve problems of the moment is to step "into the dangerous quicksands of governmental dictation."[41]

Thus, opening the door even partially to regimentation will, Hoover fears, bring on conflicts and interferences that must ultimately result in more discipline and less freedom. There is no government that can function for long part democracy and part tyranny. And, throughout *The Challenge to Liberty,* we are told that there is no need for such a duality in government.

Hoover would not agree with the motto of the 1933 Chicago Fair: Science finds—Industry applies—Man conforms. Engineer and technician that he was, Hoover nevertheless rejected the theory that in the Machine Age liberty was doomed. His Quaker background and his unfailing confidence that man does indeed have an intelligence and a will strengthened his belief that technology is merely a tool that man uses to aid him in achieving spiritual progress. To see an irreconcilable conflict between the Machine Age and liberty would be to turn away from the true meaning of liberty and to ignore the victories won by liberty over the centuries, for "in the end, both big business and machinery will vanish before freedom if that be necessary."[42] The question to Hoover is not whether liberty is workable anymore, but whether we are working conscientiously enough in its behalf.

We might question whether Hoover really believed that big business and the machine would be chosen over freedom by a nation so geared to quantitative accomplishment as America has been since the nineteenth century. Of course, he hoped, and no doubt believed, that such a choice would never have to be made. His optimistic and often somewhat naive implications in *The Challenge to Liberty* that material progress and spiritual progress are really two sides of the same coin, however, raise the question as to how clearly he saw, or wanted to see, the problem of sustaining the spiritual bases of liberty and liberalism in a nation and a world so blatantly commerical and utilitarian. Put another way—did his own idealism and optimism fog his view of things, or was he simply rationalizing reality the best way he could?

One of the arguments often put forth by defenders of Hoover's public policies during his administration is that he started, or at least had the idea for, many of the programs that were implemented during the New Deal. And it is an argument with considerable foundation. An interesting point, however, is that in indicting the New Deal's policies in *The Challenge to Liberty* as leading America down the path of socialism or worse, Hoover is, at best, on shaky philosophical ground. On the one hand, he rejects laissez faire; on the other, he rejects government interference in business and commerce. What he ends up with is a kind of compromise position in which he says that when

necessary, government does indeed have a duty to regulate; but
whatever regulation it imposes must be within the context of
liberty. And there, as we have noted before, is the catch. Hoover
does not give the impression that he sees this in any way as a
paradoxical situation. On the contrary, he takes the position that
the Constitution has proved, and will continue to prove, a brake
on efforts to destroy equality of opportunity, and that it is
flexible enough to make our economic system responsive to our
social requirements.

Hoover recognizes that in the beginning of the American
democratic experiment, the states were jealously protective of
their rights and responsibilities. He also recognizes that in his
own time many of them were "willing enough to pass difficult
questions up to Washington, or allow other states to carry the
burden of the solution. At all times we have to meet restless
members of the community who rather than slowly develop a
sense of state responsibility would rush to Washington for
mustard plaster for the whole nation."[43] The antidote, however,
is not a universal mustard plaster, but a reawakening of the
American spirit, a spirit that played so great a role in carving a
nation out of the wilderness. That, postulates Hoover, is the
antidote; for as he said at the 1936 Republican convention, "the
social order does not rest upon orderly economic freedom alone.
It rests even more upon the ideals and character of a people."[44]

Thus we must see Hoover, and more specifically *The Challenge
to Liberty,* as the product of both the spiritual and material
aspects of the American Dream. For himself, Hoover not only
reconciled these divergent aspects, he welded them together to
form a life view and a pattern of action based on that view that
made him more than an engineer and statesman. It made him a
symbol. But more of that later.

Like his other books, *The Challenge to Liberty* exhibits a
ponderous style marked by stilted phrases. Hoover uses no
specific incidents to lend an element of drama to the book, but
simply presents his ideas in solid blocks—perhaps reflecting the
gravity with which he viewed his subject. While some viewed
the book as part of an effort to gain the Republican nomination
for president or as the result of a need for self-justification,
William Allen White declared that "no one can doubt that when
the whole book has been read by the American people, they will

see in it not a political bid for power or restored prestige, but an honest man's patriotic protest against shortcuts to economic security."[45]

CHAPTER 6

America: A Moral Gibraltar

THIS chapter examines some of those views of Herbert Hoover that have led many to see him as a confirmed isolationist in terms of American foreign policy. Isolationism, of course, may be defined in many ways and in varying degrees. To label Hoover an isolationist pure and simple would be to oversimplify the position he held and, perhaps, to raise unjust questions as to his motivation in holding that position. Above all, Hoover was for building up the instrumentalities of peace and reducing the armaments of war. "This world," he said in 1932, "needs peace. It must have peace with justice. I shall continue to strive unceasingly, with every power of mind and spirit, to explore every possible path that leads toward a world in which right triumphs over force, in which reason rules over passion, in which men and women may rear their children not to be devoured by war but to pursue in safety the nobler arts of peace."[1]

Every power of mind and spirit—yes. But the power of force—no. Hoover was for the mobilization of public opinion against war and for peace, but he was against the use of force toward those ends. "We shall. . .consult with other nations in times of emergency to promote world peace. We shall enter no agreements committing us to any future course of action or which call for use of force to preserve peace."[2]

The above statements were made while Hoover was president, but in the years following his presidency, he never faltered in adhering to the basis of the position reflected in those statements. *America's First Crusade* (1941) shows this, as do a number of the speeches he gave between the years 1941 and 1953.

94

I   *Lessons of Versailles*

In late December of 1941 Hoover published the small book entitled *America's First Crusade,* based on materials that he had prepared in 1934 and 1935 for use in his memoirs. These materials dealt with the Treaty of Versailles and Hoover's part as an advisor to President Woodrow Wilson and appeared first in a series of articles for the *Saturday Evening Post* during November of 1941. In the foreword of the book, which was no doubt prepared after America's entrance into World War II, Hoover states that although he did not intend publication of the material in question during his lifetime, a friend (unidentified) convinced him that his views on the Treaty of Versailles might be of value to the American people in helping them to understand the problems faced by the world in 1941. He also points out in the foreword that the material was uninfluenced by the war.

Certainly Hoover had a unique opportunity to witness firsthand the economic problems of a continent ravaged by war, as he worked unceasingly between 1914 and 1919 to prevent starvation and to bring about a just and lasting peace.

As noted previously, Hoover was not a member of the American Peace Mission following World War I. He was, however, close to those who were. In his own mind, being a part of the mission or not was essentially unimportant. In the first chapter of *America's First Crusade,* he maintains that his own food relief organization was more in touch with the realities of Europe, both during and immediately after the war, than were any of the peace missions. "I also had," he says, "ideas as to the nature of what the Peace ought to be."[3] Basically, those ideas, as he states and restates throughout his writings and his speeches, focus on representative government as the only hope for lasting peace.

With the end of the war, American hopes were high that "the time had now come when a peace would be made which would be enduring, would end all war and, by establishing democracy over the earth, would insure that peace."[4] Such hopes were the natural outgrowth of America's views of the war as a crusade to destroy militarism and dictatorship. As Hoover points out, "We had fought far less to defeat Germany than to bring an end to aggression and war."[5] For no other reason would America violate a long tradition of nonintervention in European affairs.

Implied early in the book, then, is something that Hoover makes obvious later: that American idealism was, in the peace conference, pitted against the deception and intrigue of European pragmatism. And Woodrow Wilson was a symbol of that idealism, as he journeyed to Versailles, armed, as it were, with his Fourteen Points as the basis of a peace treaty. Indeed, the Germans had proposed the Armistice on the condition that Wilson's points would provide that basis—and the Allies had, with the exception of the point on freedom of the seas, agreed.

In reality, however, none of the Allied leaders was free to negotiate a peace in the context of Wilson's Fourteen Points, for, as Hoover writes, "destructive forces sat at the Peace Table. The life and future of 26 jealous European races were on that table. The genes of a thousand years of inbred hate and fear were in the blood of every delegation."[6] And they were present at Versailles with the delegates because they were present at home with the delegates' peoples. At such a peace table, Hoover sees Wilson as having been totally out of place. He was not sufficiently conversant with the men and forces that he came up against. Since American involvement in the war had been more detached and since Americans wanted no territory or repatriation, American statesmen, says Hoover, could rise above hatred and desire for revenge.

In the hard light of peace negotiations, European leaders simply saw American idealism as being completely out of tune with reality. America had made no great blood sacrifice; America did not have to be wary of potential enemies at her borders. Moreover, Wilson's points were seen as too vague for practical application, and Wilson himself was seen as too much the preacher, too much the missionary—delivering to the Allies little sermonettes, "full of rudimentary sentences about things which they had fought for years to vindicate when the President was proclaiming that he was too proud to fight."[7] Wilson may have been the hope for a small group of liberal peace negotiators, but for the majority he was an ineffective idealist.

Shortly after his arrival in Europe for the treaty negotiations, Wilson asked Hoover for his estimate of the situation in Paris. The latter's response was frankly negative: "I remarked that the whole air had suddenly become impregnated with currents of indescribable malignity. There had been a let-down in the whole *élan* of the war. All Europe was faced with desperation. I said I could describe these attitudes in persons as the spirits of greed, robbery, power, sadistic hate and revenge. But as applied to nations. . .or government officials, I could think of no equivalent expression."[8] Hoover relates that he was convinced that Europe looked upon America, not with deference to American views, but as the "golden-egged goose," and he so told Wilson. The latter, at the time, disagreed strongly with Hoover's estimate of the situation, but later admitted that what Hoover had said was accurate enough.

The fundamental problem that faced Wilson in the negotiations, according to Hoover, was to "set in motion forces which would sustain constructive democracy in all these nations; would get them back to work and productivity; and would bind their aspiration for peace into a workable machinery which would readjust the errors of the treaties."[9] And it was no easy task.

Hoover pictures Britain's Lloyd George as a man of considerable moral courage and physical energy, who moved in the diplomatic arena with quickness and adroitness—"as nimble as the pea in a shell-game."[10] A born leader of the mob, his major principle was expediency, particularly when the interests of Britain were directly concerned. These qualities gave him a decided advantage over Wilson, whose basic honesty and devotion to truth made him vulnerable to European diplomatic tactics.

Clemenceau of France is described as "the most utterly realistic, blunt statesman at the Peace Table."[11] Bitter at the devastation and suffering inflicted upon his nation, he viewed Wilson's Fourteen Points as "a joke on history." Force was the key principle in his mind; without it, right could never prevail. He saw democracy in Germany as a fraud and would impose such conditions on Germany that she would be utterly helpless in the years to come.

As for Orlando of Italy, his one mission was to gain territory that was promised him by Britain and France in a secret treaty made in 1915—a treaty, incidentally, that Wilson knew nothing about. Wilson's rage, upon hearing of Orlando's demands, limited Italy's territorial gains to only a few islands.

Hoover does not attack any of these leaders personally. On the contrary, he exhibits considerable respect for them and takes pains to point out that he himself was able to get along well with them. Nevertheless, they were difficult to deal with in the negotiations.

At Hoover's suggestion, Wilson appointed an economic council to keep the American peace delegation informed on economic questions that arose in the negotiations. The council consisted of Bernard Baruch, Vance McCormick, Norman Davis, Henry Robinson, and Hoover. Hoover was deeply concerned that France, Britain, and Italy were really out to take whatever advantage they could of America by proposing the issuance of League of Nations bonds, to be used for the reconstruction of Europe. The bonds were to be secured by German reparations and guaranteed by various governments, including the United States. The net effect of such a plan, Hoover saw, would make the United States the guarantor and probably payer of a large segment of German reparations.

As Hoover explains in *America's First Crusade,* he presented Wilson with the idea that he, Wilson, should set up a council and assembly of the League, with no powers other than "the right to inquire into facts, to state the facts and the broad purpose to promote the peace of the world."[12] A rather interesting idea. Hoover's theory was that too legalistic a setup of an international body damaged its real foundation—namely, cooperation. Wilson did not follow this advice because, writes Hoover, his "mind was on the Constitution of the United States to be applied to the whole earth.'[13] He goes on to say that "the light of subsequent experience shows that my line was the only practical one for the time. It would have avoided a thousand pitfalls, and would assuredly have secured American membership and support. And I believe it would have been of infinite service."[14]

With the peace efforts degenerating because of delays and machinations, Wilson came more and more to see the League Covenant to be the only real hope. But, as Hoover says, "in the creation of the League itself, the Allied powers made sure that they would surrender nothing, change nothing, by securing effective control of the Council."[15]

Hoover's own fears lay in the direction of too much American involvement in what he saw as distinctly European affairs. America wanted no reparations, no territory; and to continue membership in the several commissions set up under the peace treaty would be to sit in enforcement of the peace. So thought Hoover, and so he told Wilson in a letter dated April 11, 1919:

I have the feeling that revolution in Europe is by no means over. The social wrongs in these countries are far from solution and the tempest must blow itself out, probably with enormous violence. Our people are not prepared for us to undertake the military policing of Europe while it boils out its social wrongs. I have no doubt that if we could undertake to police the world and had the wisdom of statesmanship to see its gradual social evolution, we would be making a great contribution to civilization, but I am certain that the American people are not prepared for such a measure and I am also sure that if we remain in Europe with military force, tied in an alliance which we have never undertaken, we should be forced into this storm of repression of revolution, and forced in under terms of co-ordination with other people that would make our independence of action wholly impossible.[16]

As mentioned previously, Hoover was upset when he first saw the final draft of the peace treaty in the early hours of the morning of May 7, 1919. Nor did he feel any differently when he and his American colleagues went to the Hall of Mirrors of Versailles on June 28 of that year to witness the signing of the treaty: ". . .I had difficulty in keeping my mind on the ceremony. It was constantly traveling along the fearful consequences of many paragraphs which these men were signing with such pomp, and their effect on millions of human beings; then moving back to the high hopes with which I had landed in Europe eight months before. And I came away depressed and not exultant."[17]

Wilson's expression of American ideals was, according to Hoover, the only spiritual expression in the entire course of the peace deliberations. Though his Fourteen Points were made a shambles by European diplomacy, "he effectively tempered the march of Allied militarism on the one hand and of Bolshevism on the other. At every step he fought the forces of Hate and Imperialism."[18] And it was Wilson for whom many European nations named streets and parks and constructed monuments.

Hoover did not see the League of Nations—or its failure—as having brought calamity to the world, though there were many in America who did. The weaknesses of the League, says Hoover, were not the provisions within the covenant, but those outside of it. Britain, France, and Italy used the League as a tool for insuring

the domination over Europe that Versailles gave them, and in the
process "sowed the dragon's teeth of future revolutions and
trouble. The reparations and controls stifled German recovery
and ultimately her collapse dragged the world into economic
depression."[19] Hoover lays upon the dominant European powers
significant responsibility for preventing the growth of democracy among the defeated nations. As an example, he points to
France's negative response to his urgings (through Ambassador
Hugh Gibson) during the disarmament conference at Geneva
that some modification of the Treaty of Versailles be carried out
in order to strengthen democratic advances in the German
Republic. Had his advice been heeded, Hoover implies, Hitler's
takeover might have been prevented.

The key point that Hoover makes in *America's First Crusade*
comes in the last part of the book—and it is that point that gave
rise to much criticism of the book and of Hoover. Moving beyond
the intrigues of European diplomacy and the foibles of European
statesmen, Hoover comes to the conclusion that there were far
more powerful forces that lay behind the rejection of American
ideas at Versailles and the subsequent conferences. "Here was,"
he says, "the collision of civilizations that had grown 300 years
apart."[20]

Americans, he goes on, fail to realize how far Europe and
America have diverged—primarily because they still are overly
influenced by the sense of the historical past and rich cultural
accomplishments of Europe and, consequently, overlook the
tremendously explosive forces that are ever present among the
many European nationalities. "The areas of mixed populations,"
he sums up, "create the 'irredentas' of constant agitation and
conflict. In every one of these zones some races are separated
from their fatherlands. The existing government unceasingly
seeks to impose its national language and customs upon those
minorities. The outcries of these oppressed to the sympathies of
their racial brothers across the borders are unceasing stimulants
to friction. And these boundaries shift from every war and the
conflicts flame up in new areas."[21] The result is that Europe has
only intervals of unstable peace; and even in the periods of
peace, there is "a groping for a balance of power through groups
and alliances based upon fear and upon arms."[22]

America, on the other hand, blessed with plentiful resources,
protected by two oceans, and free from class stratifications, has

had the opportunity to develop a true democracy, an American democracy. And it is such a development that has moved America and Europe apart and has made American idealism inappropriate for the latter: "It is not strange that attempts to force the idealism of America were discarded by Europe as the solution of Europe's problems. And that idealism was proved wholly incapable of dealing with the very practical problems of Europe. Certainly we cannot impose our ideas of freedom and peace upon other people by arms or treaties."[23]

However optimistic we might think Hoover's life view was, in *America's First Crusade* he shows that he did not overlook human imperfection. Behind America's ideas of freedom, he cautions, lies a tendency to overlook the inherent weaknesses in the human animal—a tendency not prevalent among Europeans. Such a situation puts America at a disadvantage in the power politics of the diplomatic scene and may well be a significant reason for Hoover's feeling that America should keep its involvement in European affairs at a minimum: "The conflicts in concepts, the experience of the treaty-making, and our form of government should indicate how impossible it was for America to remain involved in the intimate problems of Europe. And it was the apparition of these problems that largely caused America to refuse membership in the League. It was not an unwillingness of our people to cooperate in broad measures to preserve peace."[24]

The publication of *America's First Crusade* was greeted by considerable adverse criticism, coming as it did just after the Japanese bombing of Pearl Harbor. Evidently realizing the unfortunate timing of the book, Hoover hoped to avert the sending of advance copies to the New York reviewers, but was unsuccessful. In a letter to Whitney Darrow, an editor at Scribner's (publishers of the book), he wrote, "What's done is done. I have no doubt as to the scolding that will come to this book in view of the event of December 7."[25] A little over two weeks later he wrote to Darrow that "the explosion that I prophesied has obviously appeared. The left-wingers and the Union Now people are apparently much aggravated."[26]

The explosion that Hoover mentioned was exemplified in a review by Walter Mills: "It is extraordinary that a man to whom there attaches the responsibility, no less than the honor of being an ex-President of the United States should permit the publication at this moment of a pamphlet like this. . .with the United

States locked in the death struggle declared upon us by the most savage military power in history, it becomes a piece of irresponsibility not easy to describe."[27] Mills, as did many other reviewers, saw the book as a contribution to defeatism and an insult to Britain and France. "Perhaps," wrote Llewellyn White, "one of the first things we should get rid of in preparing for the peace is this Pharisaic snobbery that assumes that our way of life is beyond the comprehension of ordinary Europeans and Asiatics and too damned good for them anyway."[28]

On the pro side, more or less, Boak Carter responded to the spate of negative comments: "If Hoover's book is truthful—and hurts—can we not accept it like men? A generation that has a rendezvous with destiny should not mind a book. A house painter has rocked the world. An American President has been elected three times. Japan attacks Hawaii, lunges to the gates of Singapore. Libya is a seesaw. Europe replaces the Bible with the sword, *Mein Kampf* and the swastika."[29]

The message of *America's First Crusade,* ill-timed or not, is not really one advocating isolationism for its own sake on the part of America. That was never part of Hoover's views. A year before the work in question, he wrote of America's role as he saw it:

There is no such thing as isolation for the United States from this war. The Monroe Doctrine itself is denial of that. And there can be no such thing as economic or intellectual or moral or spiritual isolation. There can be no isolation from world effort to allay misery, to save human life, to bring peace, disarmament, and reconstruction and renewed hope from this catastrophe. There can be isolation from military participation in this war. When I speak of joining in these wars I mean joining in the military side—sending our sons into it.

If we join in these wars we would start with the already great exhaustion of ten years of our depression. Then we will further exhaust our economic strength. And that exhaustion will be to a far greater degree than in the few months we particpated in the last war. And when the war is over we shall need devote our remaining resources to support our wounded, our maimed, our orphaned and our destitute. We shall need every resource to rebuild our farmers and workers from our own misery and impoverishment. And our sympathies will be justly limited to suffering at home.

If we join in this war the last great remaining strength will have been exhausted. And hope of world recuperation will have been delayed while Revolution marches unimpeded over the earth.

If we join in this war we ourselves will develop all the hates that are inevitable from war. We shall have lost the voice of reason in the making of peace.[30]

That much of what Hoover predicts in the above article did not come to pass is not so significant as the point that the isolation that he was talking about was really not isolation so much as military nonintervention.

Hoover did not see Americans as any more peace-loving than Europeans: "The great masses of the German people and the Russian people did not wish for the war now going on. The vast majority of these nations are gentle, decent people who prayed for peace even as did you and I."[31] Nor did he see Americans as being beyond hate. Indeed, possessing the heritage of virtually every European culture and nationality, Americans themselves could easily enough be divided in their allegiances and sympathies regarding the belligerents. But if America could remain free of the actual fighting, she could also more easily remain free of hate and thus be a beacon of reason and hope among nations that too often grope blindly through the valleys of death and destruction. This is the message of *America's First Crusade* and of so many of Hoover's speeches.

II *A Call to American Reason*

Hoover, as we have seen, was opposed to America's involvement in World War II right up to the Japanese attack on Pearl Harbor. When he spoke in a radio broadcast from Chicago on June 29, 1941, Germany had just invaded Russia and America was getting more deeply involved in providing England with war materiel and food supplies. Moreover, there were those who saw the United States already in the war. In response to such a view, Hoover reminded his audience that only Congress can declare war. He went on to charge Congress with the responsibility of seeing that the nation did not become involved in an undeclared war. Such a statement was probably made in response to those actions of President Roosevelt that Hoover felt were drawing the nation closer and closer to the brink.

In the face of the uncertain situation facing the nation, Hoover, as we might expect, pointed to "certain courses of practical statesmanship" and "certain eternal principles to which we must adhere."[32] One thing Hoover no doubt had in mind was the constant necessity to contain what he described as the "militant Communist conspiracy against the whole democratic ideals of the world."[33] Russia's forced entry into the war would serve Britain well and vice versa, but it would make America's joining the war to defend the freedoms of mankind a "gargantuan jest."

In the activities of Communist Russia since the end of World War I Hoover saw nothing but a hideous record of violations of treaties and international law. Such violations led to the enslavement of a number of nations that America had helped along the democratic path following that war. Aligning ourselves with Russia would be as great a violation of our ideals as aligning ourselves with Hitler. After all, did not Russia and Germany join forces to take for themselves Poland, Latvia, Estonia, and Lithuania, democracies (more or less) which the United States had aided and encouraged since their inception? So reasoned Hoover.

The conclusion that Hoover reached was that America should stand aside and allow Hitler and Stalin to exhaust themselves against each other. As the only remaining sanctuary of freedom, America should aid Britain and China but should not "put the American flag or American boys in the zone of war. Arm to the teeth for defense of the Western Hemisphere, and cease to talk and to provoke war. Uphold Congress steadily in assuming the responsibility to determine peace or war. Stop this notion of ideological war to impose the four freedoms on other nations by military force and against their will. Devote ourselves to improving the four freedoms within our borders that the light of their success may stir the peoples of the world to their adoption."[34] His comments in this speech, while marked by gravity, are hopeful; but then Hoover was never a man given to despair. His optimism, however, was tempered by realism.

In 1954 he recalled his advice to let Hitler and Stalin exhaust each other: "I stated that the result of our assistance would be to spread Communism over the whole world. I urged that if we stood aside the time would come when we could bring lasting peace to the world. I have no regrets. The consequences have proved that I was right."[35]

Hindsight, of course, may make the ideas Hoover presented in this speech seem more plausible and appropriate than they did to the nation in 1941, caught up as it was with the psychosis of war. Whatever, his comments reflect with cogent accuracy his view of America as a nation with a unique practical and spiritual mission in the world.

In December of 1949 Senator William Knowland of California asked Hoover for his views on the China situation. The ironies of war and international diplomacy had turned an ally into a potential enemy. China was divided, with Mao Tse-tung and the Communists on the mainland and Chiang Kai-shek and the Nationalists on Formosa. We should not be surprised that Hoover, in a letter to Knowland, came out strongly against the recognition of the Communist government and just as strongly in favor of support for Chiang. Among his reasons were containment of communism in the Pacific, prevention of another Communist permanent member of the United Nations Security Council, maintenance of symbolic resistance as a basis for saving Southeastern Asia, and continued hope of someday turning China back to the path of democracy.

Hoover never slackened in his opposition to Red China or in his support of Formosa and Chiang. Again, as to recognition of Red China, he wrote in 1950 that "we might bear in mind that in eleven years—from 1933 to 1944—we either 'recognized' or acquiesced in the annexation of some fourteen nations made Communist. From the first day to this we have had nothing from any of them but attacks, defamation of our country, conspiracies against our internal order, and opposition to every effort to bring peace to the world."[36] In 1954 he spoke out again, this time against the admission of Red China to the United Nations. To Hoover, Red China represented, as did all Communist countries, a source of gigantic evil and posed a dire threat to the peace and safety of the world.

Hoover often pointed to the years after 1933 as years in which American statesmanship, particularly with regard to communism, was in some disarray. There was no question in his mind that recognition of Soviet Russia in 1933 was a tragic mistake, and he placed the blame on what he called "our left wingers." "They produced," he said on April 27, 1950, "the recognition of the Soviet in 1933. They produced the alliance with Russia in 1941. They produced the appeasement of Russia in Western Europe until its reversal by President Truman and Secretary Byrnes in

1945. I will not join in the explanations about China. Up to now
there is agreement on only one point. We lost the game—
400,000,000 to nothing."[37]

As a result of this lost statesmanship, America found herself in
a cold war—bitter proof that the "one-world idea seems to be
lost in the secret files."[38] It was really two worlds pitted against
each other—one holding to militarism, imperialism, and atheism
and rejecting compassion; the other believing in God, freedom,
the dignity of man, and peace. Hoover never had a problem
defining the polarities of any issue. He saw America's burden
growing ever larger in the effort to withstand the ceaseless
onslaughts of communism and made a plea for a "spiritual
mobilization of the nations who believe in God against this tide of
Red agnosticism."[39]

In an address at Emporia, Kansas, on July 11, 1950, Hoover
pointed out that the goal of a lasting peace was no less elusive
following World War II than it was following World War I.
Viewing Russia as a great malignant force standing in the way of
peace, he called for a reexamination of America's experience in
two world wars as a way to certain truths. The first truth was that
war cannot change ideas; people must do that. A second was that
it is a mistake to concentrate on winning battles; strategy must
always be directed toward winning a peace. A third was that to
resist the spirit of imperialism, vindictiveness and revenge must
be resisted. And finally a fourth was that lasting peace can come
only when accompanied by disarmament. The implication is that
these truths were not realized by America's statesmen, or by any
other nation's statesmen, for that matter.

While admitting that the United Nations faced a most difficult
task, he still saw that organization as the one best hope. The
alternative would be "to crawl into isolation and defend the
Western Hemisphere alone. That would be less than a secure
peace."[40] But, as he said several months later in New York,
America cannot carry the entire burden of Western civilization;
Europe must do its share. And that point Hoover would have
made quickly and clearly. If Europe fails to understand that the
American economy cannot long stand the strain of the above
burden, then "we had better quit talking and paying, and
consider holding the Atlantic Ocean with Britain (if they wish) as
one frontier, and the Pacific Ocean with an armed Japan and
other islands as the other frontier."[41] Whether Hoover really

believed such could be done or whether he was merely emphasizing a point, we can only guess. But such a statement echoes those made on other occasions when Hoover cautioned that American ideals are often not compatible with European diplomacy. Moreover, he never wavered in his belief that America, because of those ideals, stood above other nations of the world.

Two months after he warned that America could not alone defend Europe, Hoover made another radio address (December 20, 1950) from New York in answer, he said, to hundreds of requests that he "appraise the present situation and give my conclusions as to our national policies."[42] There is no question that Hoover felt a deep sense of responsibility regarding the world situation of the time and also no question that he welcomed any opportunlity he could get to talk on that situation.

The picture that he presented in this address was that of a gigantic Communist military machine poised for a thrust from Russia into Western Europe and from China into Southeastern Asia. Russia herself may have continued in her paranoia of seeing herself surrounded by enemies on all sides, but Hoover saw her as a powerful adversary, willing and capable of advancing communism militantly. He concluded that in any land war the Russians would win—or at least could not be defeated; that even with their superior manpower the Russians could not invade the United States; that the atomic bomb in such a situation was a far less dominant weapon than once thought; and that the United Nations had been defeated in Korea by the Chinese aggressors.

With the above conclusions as a base, Hoover, ever the engineer, proposed seven principles of action:

1. The foundation of our national policies must be to preserve for the world this Western Hemisphere Gibraltar of Western Civilization.

2. We can, without any measure of doubt, with our own air and naval forces, hold the Atlantic and Pacific oceans with one frontier on Britain (if she wishes to cooperate); the other, on Japan, Formosa and the Philippines. We can hold open the sea lanes for our supplies.

And I devoutly hope that a maximum of cooperation can be established between the British Commonwealth and ourselves.

3. To do this we should arm our air and naval forces to the teeth. We have little need for large armies unless we are going to Europe or China. We should give Japan her independence and aid her in arms to defend herself. We should stiffen the defenses of our Pacific frontier in

Formosa and the Philippines. We can protect this island chain by our sea and air power.

4. We could, after initial outlays for more air and navy equipment, greatly reduce our expenditures, balance our budget and free ourselves from the dangers of inflation and economic degeneration.

5. If we toil and sacrifice as the President has so well asked, we can continue aid to the hungry of the world. Out of our productivity, we can give aid to other nations when they have already displayed spirit and strength in defense against communism. We have the stern duty to work and sacrifice to do it.

6. We should have none of appeasement. Morally there is no appeasement of communism. Appeasement contains more dangers than Dunkirks. We want no more Teherans and no more Yaltas. We can retrieve a battle but we cannot retrieve an appeasement. We are grateful that President Truman has denounced such a course.

7. We are not blind to the need to preserve Western civilization on the Continent of Europe or to our cultural and religious ties to it. But the prime obligation of defense of Western Continental Europe rests upon the nations of Europe. The test is whether they have the spiritual force, the will and acceptance of unity among them by their own volition. America cannot create their spiritual forces; we cannot buy them with money.[43]

Throughout his career, Hoover often displayed an impatience with Europe's fears and disunities, and he did so again in the above speech. Remarking once more on the sacrifices that America made in two wars to save Europe, he urged a cessation of any more aid until Europeans manifested more spiritual strength and unity—more desire—to draw upon their own resources to defend themselves.

Probably realizing that such statements would bring upon him the indictment of isolationism, he quickly described his suggested policies as not isolationist, but really the opposite of isolationism: "They would avoid rash involvement of our military forces in hopeless campaigns. They do not relieve us of working to our utmost. They would preserve a stronghold of Christian civilization in the world against any peradventure."[44] The image of an America standing as a Gibraltar for all that is good and decent in the world may seem naive and trite to some—but not to Herbert Hoover. For him it was a basic truth.

CHAPTER 7

Not Victory Alone

TO incumbent presidents, living ex-presidents may seem a nuisance on occasion, especially if they are of a different party. Certainly the feelings between Herbert Hoover and Franklin Roosevelt were not marked by amiability, and probably few thought it strange that the latter never once called upon Hoover for aid during the three and one-half years that the United States was at war. To say that Hoover would have welcomed an opportunity to play some official role in the nation's war effort would no doubt be an understatement. Although he had no such opportunity offered him, he still had an effective way to make his views known—writing. As we have seen, his experience during World War I and the peace negotiations that followed had left a deep impression upon Hoover. He knew well that any war can be divided into two parts—the fighting of the war and the making of peace. And the second part for Hoover was just as important over the long run as the first. Along with his friend Hugh Gibson, who had had thirty years of government experience, including duties at the Versailles Peace Conference, Hoover had strong feelings regarding peace efforts that would be required following the current war. Together, they wrote *The Problems of Lasting Peace* (1942), to be followed two years later by *The Basis of Lasting Peace* (1944).

I *Dynamic Forces of Peace and War*

Hoover and Gibson, in *The Problems of Lasting Peace*, point to seven dynamic forces that they see as having largely shaped the history of the world. These forces will, moreover, continue to shape the world—particularly in terms of their implications for the problems of war and peace. They are ideologies; economic pressures; nationalism; imperialism; militarism; fear, with its consequences of hate and revenge; and the will to peace.

Ideological forces—religious, social, economic, political, artistic, and scientific ideas—have over the centuries made considerable impact on the history of the world. While the crusading spirit inherent in ideologies has often caused man to raise the sword in their behalf, these same ideologies can also be instrumental in achieving and maintaining peace. Hoover and Gibson see Christianity and the concepts of personal liberty and representative government as having peace as their ultimate goal. The problem, as they ascertain it, is that the new ideologies of Nazism, fascism, and communism are more aggressive than that of personal liberty. The latter, therefore, must be infused with a new spirit and raised once more to crusading heights.

Hoover and Gibson do not profess a faith in the theories of economic determinism, yet the very fact that men must have food, clothing, and shelter make economic forces and pressures eternal. More than that, however, these forces have been expanded to become a prime cause of imperialism—particularly in the modern world, where the search for raw materials and for markets to sell finished products "have led to incessant friction, hate, fear, and war."[1] Hoover saw as early as 1919 that the economic aftermaths that were forced upon Germany would in all probability result in another world conflagration.

Nationalism, according to Hoover and Gibson, is one of the deepest of man's instincts and emotions, gathering "from a thousand springs of common race with its common language, religion, folklore, traditions, literature, art, music, beliefs, habits, modes of expression, hates, fears, ideals, and tribal loyalties."[2] Because it is so deep-seated in man, nationalism has been the cause of numerous wars of independence, as one group after another has gone through trial by fire in an effort to achieve self-determination. Neither victory nor defeat will lessen the spirit of nationalism. On the contrary, "it is fired to greater heat by every war and every peacemaking. A fiercer nationalism flares out of every defeat and every victory."[3] Though they see extreme nationalism (imperialism) as a dangerous force, Hoover and Gibson do not reject nationalism generally. In its best sense, it is a satisfaction and a fulfillment and can give rise to better government and a spiritual and social unity among a people. But whatever its results, nationalism is a force that will be present in the world as long as man is present.

If nationalism is deep-seated in man, so too is militarism. A combative and egoistic creature who loves a contest, man is prone to transform his feelings of superiority into arrogance and thence into aggression. Moreover, say Hoover and Gibson, there is in some races a definite aggressive warrior strain that glorifies war for its own sake; and they point to Germany and Japan as examples—particularly Germany, perhaps because "unlike the French and the Britons, they were never conquered by the Romans and given the advantages of that form of education"[4] And there are also what Hoover and Gibson call the Pied Pipers—those men who, consumed with ambition, call upon their countrymen to embark on campaigns of conquest.

Closely related to militarism, of course, is imperalism, which Hoover and Gibson define as "the movement of races over their racial borders."[5] This may seem a rather delimiting definition; but the authors, in their discussion, broaden it considerably, recognizing that, in modern times, imperialism has had primarily an economic motivation. Even democracies have had their imperialistic tendencies—yet, "wherever imperialism has been successful over long periods, it has always rested upon class government."[6] While imperialism is easily one of the major causes of war, Hoover and Gibson give it little credit as an instrument of peace, even though it "has been present in every peacemaking, and it will be there next time."[7]

The forces of fear, hate, and revenge are the very ones that Hoover was cautioning against in the peace negotiations following World War I. Humiliation usually accompanies defeat; and, if that humiliation is burned even more deeply into the collective soul of a nation with the hot iron of vengeance, hate quickly replaces it. Such hate breeds new wars, and the vicious circle is once more joined.

Having thus far painted a rather grim picture of the forces that militate against peace in the world, Hoover and Gibson do offer one hope: the will to peace that is ever in the background of men's minds. In the midst of the excitement and glory and sense of mission that marks the beginning of most wars, it is easy to overlook the infinite suffering of war. It is not long, however, before the horror of war is made graphically apparent through grief, poverty, moral degeneration, destruction, and death. No wonder, then, that men for centuries have searched for the secret to permanent peace, albeit unsuccessfully. "And indeed,"

Hoover and Gibson ironically note, "the spiritual concepts of peace have brought it to pass that every war must be justified by its leaders as a war of defense and for the one purpose of securing peace. And the end of every war is received with joy and the ringing of church bells."[8]

II   The Path to Total War

In terms of the problems of war and peace for the world at the time they were writing, Hoover and Gibson view the 165 years since the American and French revolutions as having great significance. History cannot, as Hoover and Gibson recognize, be divided neatly into periods; nor can causes of wars be traced definitively and sequentially back through history to a single source or event. Nevertheless, the period which they choose to examine was one marked by tremendous pressures exerted by the seven dynamic forces previously mentioned.

The 140 years between the above-mentioned revolutions and the explosion of World War I saw two ideologies contending for dominance in the world—the concept of personal liberty as made manifest by representative government against the concept of the precedence of the state over the individual. In this context, personal liberty and representative government made considerable gains throughout the Western world, to the extent that subjection of the individual was primarily a matter of social and economic class. War, however, is anathema to personal liberty, and World War I exacted a heavy price in terms of the surrender of personal freedoms—thus underscoring what Hoover had said previously in *The Challenge to Liberty:* that liberty needs peace to flourish.

During this same period, the Industrial Revolution turned civilization more and more toward materialism. The Virgin indeed gave way to the Dynamo,[9] as the predominantly religious and spiritual character of earlier times was pushed into the background in favor of the philosophies of such economists as Adam Smith. Hoover and Gibson trace this development to the impulses of economic freedom, which itself stemmed from the ideas of personal liberty. Free minds produced scientific research and inventions that improved production, transportation, and communication—culminating in great aggregations of capital and finance. In short, modern capitalism. Undaunted, the authors see this dramatic shift in the bases of civilization in a most optimistic light:

From these developments of technology and of mechanical power came a vast increase in the productivity of man, an unparalleled rise in the standard of living and comfort among all civilized races. And in turn, from these resources came an expansion of the humanities. Art and music were made accessible to all; literature flourished; science developed rapidly; education was widespread; public health was studied and improved; and there were a thousand lesser manifestations of this trend. This progress and the constantly wider spread of intellectual, spiritual, and political freedom filled the hearts of men with hope and confidence. Men moved almost everywhere over the earth without fear or passports. Indeed, the last quarter of a century before the first World War may have been the golden age of good living. Certainly, despite the turn toward materialism, it was an age of confidence and hope.[10]

With the golden age, however, came problems. The intense and complex economic system brought about by the Machine Age was marked by a rhythm of production and consumption that resulted in boom-slump cycles that, in turn, gave rise to speculation, greed, and misery. And personal liberty, too, was periodically threatened by large groups and organizations that tried to stifle competition and to influence, or even control, government. Even so, Hoover and Gibson see such weaknesses and clashes in the economic system as having less to do with causing World War I than they did with the degeneration that followed that war. They point to other economic pressures, though, that did play an important role in igniting the conflict— namely, "the pressures of intensified populations in manufacturing countries for elbow room and markets."[11] These pressures in turn stimulated imperialism and militarism and drove "power politics into every corner of the world."[12]

While Spain and Portugal declined as empires during this period, Great Britain, France, Russia, Germany, Austria-Hungary, and Japan reflected considerable imperialistic growth. Even the United States more than tripled in area. Imperialism was indeed a force to be reckoned with, and as such gave rise to militarism.

France and Germany were the most obvious examples of this militarism, led by Napoleon and Frederick the Great. Other countries, too, developed powerful military establishments that had no other *raison d'être* than the waging of war. "The chips on all these shoulder-straps," say Hoover and Gibson, "and the stupid, arrogant, and aggressive minds that flaunted them gave warning that powder trains were being laid for the gigantic explosion of 1914."[13]

At the same time that imperialism and militarism were essential characteristics of a number of world powers, there were, ironically enough, considerable advances made in the direction of preserving peace. Hoover and Gibson recognize that some of these were based on military force, to be sure; but they also emphasize that some were based upon the pacific means of law, morals, and reason. In this latter category they place the Holy Alliance and the Quadruple Alliance of 1815, the Monroe Doctrine of 1823, the Hague Conferences, the concept of the balance of power, and the Concert of Europe.

While the Holy Alliance was simply a kind of agreement among sovereigns that they would be guided by the sacred principles of Christianity, the Quadruple Alliance was an elaboration of this agreement into a treaty signed by Great Britain, Prussia, Austria, and Russia, the purpose of which was to maintain a coalition against France and to set up periodic meetings to adopt measures for preserving peace in Europe. Hoover and Gibson see it as having had the clear aim of preserving the doctrine of legitimacy, which had been seriously threatened by revolution. Thus, while it helped to maintain peace, it also suppressed liberalism and nationalism.

From the congresses called under the auspices of the Quadruple Alliance evolved the principle of the balance of power in Europe. It was not a principle of law, according to Hoover and Gibson, but "a principle of action with the claim that it was a law of nature. Its essential base was to maintain a situation where nations modify their aggressiveness by fear of defeat. Fear of defeat always modifies aggressiveness—even in the jungle."[14] They see it as a positive step in the efforts toward peace because it "recognized the collective right of Europe to peace and freedom from territorial aggression."[15] And while it might not have been called into operation to resist military invasion, "the fear of its operation gives it a long record of successful retarding of such aggression."[16] History, moreover, has proven Hoover and Gibson correct in their estimation that the balance of power concept will always remain alive, not merely in a European context but in a world-wide context.

To the Concert of Europe, which was not a treaty but a practice that had its roots in the Quadruple Alliance, Hoover and Gibson attribute the prevention of war in Europe from 1870 to 1914. It was simply a more or less informal procedure of consultation among the nations in an effort to defuse crises and to bring order to the processes of international life. "It was," according to Hoover and Gibson, "a precarious way of keeping the peace, and there was always danger that the system would fail. And when it did finally fail in 1914, the failure was due to the accumulation of explosive forces beyond the powers of this form of diplomacy. Or at least statesmanship was so weak as to fail to recognize them."[17]

Hoover and Gibson view the Monroe Doctrine as an example of maintaining peace through the use of force—America's version of the balance of power concept. Both America and Britain stood behind the doctrine, each for its own reasons; but the force they together represented was sufficient to make the doctrine effective. The authors see the doctrine not only as an attempt to keep European powers out of the Western Hemisphere, but also as a reaction to the Holy Alliance's defense of Divine Right. As Hoover emphasized in *American Individualism* and *The Challenge to Liberty*, American liberty and liberalism are diametrically opposed to such a concept. Still, Hoover and Gibson, in the present work, recognize that the United States carried the doctrine too far on occasion, intervening diplomatically and militarily in various countries, thus engendering fears of, and resentment toward, our motives. It was Hoover himself who ordered the marines out of Nicaragua and Haiti and repudiated the whole thesis of intervention.

In discussing the development of law and international cooperation, Hoover and Gibson credit the spread of representative government as having a salient influence on that development. They see a direct correlation between the popular share in government and the popular demand for orderly methods in the conduct of international diplomacy. "The first fundamental and courageous attack upon the world problems of peace and war," they maintain, "was made by the Hague Peace Conference, called in 1899 by the Emperor of Russia."[18] This conference and others that preceded and followed it illustrate a distinct shift from the older conception of diplomacy, with its emphasis on alliances, intrigues, and social contracts, to a new conception of preventing disagreements and controversies—or at least defusing those that do occur before they exploded into war.

Unfortunately, this effort of the will to peace was not strong enough to withstand the pressures from the other six forces— ideologies; economic pressures; nationalism; imperialism; militarism; and fear, hate, and revenge—and the world in 1914 was plunged into a war that was to change much more than mere boundaries.

In speculating on the question of whether higher levels of statesmanship on the part of the European powers might have prevented, or at least deferred, World War I, Hoover and Gibson conclude that, while there are many instances where the finger of "only if" may be pointed, it is doubtful if enough support for the will to peace could have been rallied to do much good. Although the authors do not go so far as to say so, perhaps, more than anything else, it was a case of the desire for war overshadowing any concern for the results of war—probably because the statesmen did not realize that, since the Franco-Prussian War of the 1870s, the art of war had changed. No more was it to be fought by only a fraction of the population of a nation with only a minor disruption of economic and social life.

Total war brought with it a new ideology, according to Hoover and Gibson, an ideology that was contributed to by representative government itself:

Representative government itself contributed to the beginnings of a malevolent and hostile ideology. In order to mobilize the whole energies of their peoples, all governments at war had to plan and enforce production and to divert men and material to war purposes. They were compelled to restrict production for civilian purposes. Governments had to operate industry and dictate to business, labor, and agriculture. And where men claimed old personal rights, they had to be coerced. All this was as much needed in the countries of liberty as in those accustomed to subjection. Thus, representative government everywhere surrendered economic and personal freedom to the state that they might win the war. Government management of economic life during the war was assisted greatly by the fact that altruism and patriotism replaced self-interest as the basis of economic production and service. But the world at that spot laid the foundations of "managed economy," and thus the economics of a new ideology— Fascism.[19]

Moreover, total war, because it required government-organized propaganda, corrupted the spirit of intellectual freedom. Telling lies was justified on the premise that it saved the lives of many of a country's soldiers. Intolerance was an obvious result of propaganda.

The primary challenge to the world's leaders at the end of hostilities in 1918, at least in one sense, was not the drafting of a peace treaty so much as it was to assuage the hate and desire for revenge that enveloped the minds of the millions of civilians who had suffered war's brutalities—brutalities which, Hoover and Gibson emphasize, were more hideous than those of any preceding war:

Total war was a war of civilian effort against civilian effort as well as of armies against armies. Therefore, to dislocate civilian activities on the enemy side became a part of military action. Thus, it became also a war of armies against civilians. No longer was there chivalry of armed men for women and children. Starvation of nations brought not only agony to civilians, but stunting of their children and decimation of millions from inevitable pestilence. Terrorization of civilians was organized as an act of war. Towns were burned by the Germans as warnings, and innocent hostages were mowed down by machine guns. Airplanes and zeppelins were used to drop iron and fire upon helpless civilians, to burn their homes and their cities. Civilian sailors were sunk by submarines without a chance of survival.[20]

Such a mode of war made it virtually impossible for any statesman to work for peace short of total victory, even though, as Hoover and Gibson point out, the moment for such a negotiated peace was ripe in 1916. Had a negotiated peace been achieved at that time, the world would have been a vastly different place; and World War II, moreover, might have been avoided, or at least delayed.

Few men have known the horrible consequences spawned by the brutalities of total war as well as did Hoover. His work with the Belgian Relief presented him with a graphic picture of the suffering inflicted upon civilians. Yet Hoover and Gibson see one positive side to this—and that is the willingness of people to alleviate suffering. Hoover's own Quaker background and his idealistic view of mankind would not let him sink into the quagmire of cynicism and pessimism, even in the midst of the carnage and destruction of a world war.

III   *Armistice and Peacemaking, 1918-19*

Though we have seen that a strong vein of idealism and optimism ran through Herbert Hoover, we must nevertheless recognize that he was not totally naive. In *The Problems of Lasting Peace* he and Gibson envision no period of history when the seven dynamic forces previously discussed will ever be eliminated. The problem in preventing war or in making peace, then, is the same; namely, to control those forces leading to war and to nurture those leading to peace. Some of these forces, say Hoover and Gibson, with regard to World War I, "were altered during the progress of the war. Some were altered as a consequence of the war. But they were all in action the day after the Armistice, and, for that matter, always will be this side of the millenium. And statesmen are too often dominated by the less peaceful ones."[21]

Hoover and Gibson are not concerned in *The Problems of Lasting Peace* with "the drama of peace negotiations, the gilded halls, the pomp and circumstance surrounding these scores of nations with their celebrated representatives and their protocols of politeness, but with what they describe as "the grim unseen forces which haunted the halls of peace and shaped the coming world."[22]

The image presented by Hoover and Gibson of the American peace negotiators, headed by President Woodrow Wilson, as they sailed for Europe is one of naiveté. Their confidence that victory in the war had at last brought the opportunity for freedom to mankind and for a lasting peace was based on a concept of the world situation—Europe's situation especially—that was not in touch with reality. America's development, based on unlimited resources and the security of two oceans, had taken the nation down a far different path than that traveled by Europe. As Hoover pointed out in *American Individualism,* American liberty and liberalism were unique. But when Woodrow Wilson attempted to insert ideas of this liberty and liberalism into the peace negotiations, he ran into grimly practical European negotiators who followed the tried principles of power diplomacy: "It was the process with which over the centuries they had dealt with a hundred European crises. Their representatives belonged to classes and schools which had been born to this profession. They practiced the art with skill that comes from centuries of inheritance and training. Their formulae were seasoned in the history of Europe. The shades of Machiavelli, Marlborough, Pitt, Castlereagh, Talleyrand were all about in their spiritual descendants. To them, this was simply another crisis and no crusade of idealists. They were not impressed—below the skin at least."[23]

Still, there was some acceptance, even if only temporary, of American ideas. Certainly one of the results of the war was an immediate strengthening of representative government. Joining such nations as Britain, France, Italy, Belgium, Sweden, Norway, Holland, Denmark, Switzerland, and Greece—which already had a history of representative government—were the liberated peoples of Finland, Latvia, Estonia, Lithuania, Poland, Czechoslovakia, Rumania, Croatia, Serbia, and Slovenia. all of whom adopted governments based on representation and personal liberty. It did, indeed, seem as if "the freedom of men had triumphed over almost all the civilized world."[24]

In discussing the League of Nations, Hoover and Gibson do not view it as having ever been seen by thoughtful Americans as vital to peace. Representative government was the key: "It was the American belief that these newly freed peoples, if able to act, would refuse to stand for militarism and the burdens of aggressive arms or to vote themselves into war—except against attack. But their ability to assert themselves in this peaceful sense depended upon growth of the tender plants of representative government and personal liberty which had sprung up with the Armistice in the old militaristic areas. A chief purpose of the League, as we saw it then, was to safeguard the growth of these forces of freedom."[25]

Ironically, however, Hoover and Gibson see the Treaty of Versailles as having worked to considerable degree in the opposite direction. Instead of charging the wrongs to the ruling castes of Prussia and Austria-Hungary, for example, the Allied governments demanded their pound of flesh from the people of the enemy states. The German people, the authors point out, felt they were surrendering on the basis of Woodrow Wilson's points, but these points were never fully extended to Germany. Forcing the Germans to sign a war-guilt clause that lay a burden of guilt for causing the war upon a whole nation; maintaining a food blockade against Germany after the Armistice; levying tremendous reparations ($40 billion) upon Germany; and fragmenting

the German race by territorial changes and prohibition of union
with Austria—all were further examples of the hate-revenge
complex that motivated Allied negotiators. Nor did the treaty do
anything to alleviate the chaos resulting from the breakdown of
the economic systems of the great empires. On the contrary, say
Hoover and Gibson, the economic strains were increased.

It is not surprising that accompanying the freedom of
previously oppressed national groups came a rise in nationalism—another of the political realities of Europe for which
Americans had little comprehension. Hoover and Gibson remind
us that an often obscure line marks "where advantageous
development of national spirit ends and selfish destructive
nationalism begins. Certain it is that at once every one of these
new governments organized an army. They occupied the utmost
boundaries that they could secure. They fell into a multitude of
conflicts among themselves over how far their racial or historic
or economic boundaries should extend. Thus the nations and
boundaries of Europe were mainly determined before the peace
conference could even convene."[26] The authors, moreover, see
the same phenomenon occurring at the next peace (following
World War II), for the rights to freedom and self-determination
are concepts that fan the fires of nationalism. Peacemakers must
thus be prepared to deal with this reality.

Imperialism as a force was also very much present during and
after the peace negotiations, as the empires of Britain, France,
Belgium, and Japan grew significantly in terms of territory and
inhabitants. The authors remind us, however, that the United
States got nothing and wanted nothing.

Hoover and Gibson conclude that the Treaty of Versailles was
essentially a failure, at least insofar as having any real positive
impact on the forces that so often lead to war. True, the will to
peace brought forth the noble experiment of the League of
Nations, but the hopes for success of this experiment were
blunted in the years following Versailles.

IV   Hindsight after Versailles

The period between 1919 and 1939 was certainly one of the
more turbulent periods in the world's history—so turbulent that
the statesmanship available was unable to stem the forces that
were inexorably leading to World War II. Hopes for a new era of

peace and freedom for mankind were dashed against the rocks of Fascist and Communist dictatorships, as there occurred "the almost total revolt from Liberalism on the Continent, not only in form, but in the beliefs of men."[27] And, with the exception of Spain and Russia, it was a bloodless revolt. The Treaty of Versailles did not diminish the forces that lead to war.

Imperialism, punishment, and reparations may have shorn Germany of her possessions, but Hitler was soon to be leading the German people on an imperialistic march that eventually gave them control over vast areas of Europe. Russia and Japan were to move to enlarge their empires also. Militarism, obviously, was rampant, with the annual arms expenditure reaching from $4 billion to $18 billion between 1932 and 1938.

On the economic side, the situation was no less grim. The war, as Hoover and Gibson are quick to point out, had thrown the delicate and complicated machine-age economic system into turmoil. They trace the movement from the immediate postwar efforts to free economics from government management to the conscious or unconscious reversion to regimented economics as a way out of the morass of disorganization, bringing about "what can perhaps be defined as another ideology—that is what is called 'managed economy.' Its essential characteristic is an attempt to maintain personal liberty and representative government with some considerable degree of totalitarian methods in the field of economic freedom."[28]

As Hoover argued before, it was not a matter of all government economic regulation being bad, but a matter of degree. The problem, of course, is to recognize that point at which government regulation begins to stifle competition and to cut into the marrow of personal liberty. In all of his comments on the economic system of free enterprise, Hoover emphasizes the importance of voluntary cooperative action and security from fear, both of which are based on the confidence of the men who operate such a system. It is an illusion, he and Gibson posit,

that there can be totalitarian (or coercive) economics and at the same time a survival of the personal liberties of free speech, free press, free assembly, freedom of worship, and free representative government. The moment that managed economy steps over the line where voluntary action, co-operative movement, and individual initiative reign, protest begins. Soon the bureaucracy loses patience with opposition and starts limiting personal expression by direct or indirect coercion. Moreover, when the voters in large numbers become dependent upon the state, the rule of the majority may become tyranny.[29]

Hoover recognized as early as 1919 that American economic health was tied to that of Europe. In a speech on October 13, 1919, in San Francisco, he remarked that "with Europe in a state of economic collapse, and we, on the other hand, with a surplus of commodities in the United States to the value of perhaps three billion dollars, are looking for a market, and we just as much require that Europe shall be enabled to purchase these commodities if we are not to suffer doubly from the economic shock of war."[30] And in *The Problems of Lasting Peace* he and Gibson see Europe as the "real detonator" of the economic collapse of 1931, which dragged the United States deeper into the slough of depression.

With the dynamic forces that so often lead to war so rigorous, where was the will to peace? Hoover and Gibson describe the period in question as, on the one hand, exhibiting mankind's greatest efforts toward peace. On the other hand, however, the divergent attitudes and degenerations in relations among nations were to undermine such efforts. Placing primary blame on French leadership, the authors see France as "the stumbling block to every proposal for world advancement, constantly demanding guarantees for her own security as the price of cooperation with other nations in any direction. At the same time, she alienated her major and natural allies, Italy and Britain."[31]

Despite the many negative factors operating in the twenty years following Versailles, Hoover and Gibson see, even in the failure of the League of Nations, some lessons in the efforts to insure a lasting peace in the world. They see two areas in which the League was successful: settling a number of disputes peacefully and bringing about nonpolitical cooperation concerning human welfare. These successes, of course, were heartening because they reflected more advancement along those lines than occurred in all of the nineteenth century. But even in the causes of failure, the authors recognize valuable lessons, if for no other reason than that they illustrate those pitfalls to be avoided in the future. They list six causes of the League's failure:

Areas of Failure in League Operation
The areas of failure are no less instructive. The causes of failure lay in:
1. The survival of power diplomacy.
2. The inability to formulate a European policy of peaceful reconstruction.
3. The total collapse of the force methods in practical application.
4. The failure to secure disarmament.
5. The failure of effort or real intent to revise the onerous treaties and thus make the readjustments between nations which the injustices of the Versailles Treaty, and other treaties marking the end of the war, and normal change constantly required. That failure permitted the growth of an accumulation of conflicts and grievances, with war as the only available solvent.
6. Internal weaknesses in the League structure.[32]

V   *Foundations of Lasting Peace*

Hoover and Gibson emphasize in *The Problems of Lasting Peace* that they are not laying out a specific plan for peace, but are pointing to principles that, according to the lessons of history, must be considered if an effective and lasting peace is to be achieved. Starting from the premise that the seven dynamic forces previously discussed will be present at any peace table, they suggest fifty specific conclusions that they see emerging from humanity's long struggle with these forces: "We may perhaps be a mite critical that most thought is being devoted to alternative architectural forms of the temple rather than to the foundations. And many who contemplate the nature of the foundations assume that, because the pressure and strains are great and strong, they must be inexorable and little can be done about them. If we enter into the drafting room in this despair, we may as well accept the utter futility of all human efforts to keep the peace."[33]

The following represents a paraphrasing of the fifty conclusions reached by Hoover and Gibson:

1. War aims and the principles of peace must be reduced to specific and practical terms.
2. A foundation of political, territorial, economic, military, and ideological settlements must be carefully laid.

3. Personal liberty must replace totalitarianism.

4. Representative government is the best hope for lasting peace.

5. Liberty does not derive from force; it must be cultivated.

6. At least the forms of representative government must be accepted by the enemy states.

7. The principle of representative government must be initiated and nurtured for long years in enemy states.

8. Relief must be extended immediately to enemy states.

9. Governments of the world must assume the responsibility for relief of both liberated and defeated nations.

10. Economic freedom must be regulated to prevent abuse.

11. International trade should be restored to free enterprise.

12. Domestic free enterprise must not be stifled.

13. Except for stabilization purposes, governments should not buy and sell in foreign markets.

14. There must be monetary stability.

15. Privileged trade agreements should be abolished.

16. All trade quotas should be abolished.

17. Monopolies and cartels should be prohibited.

18. Tariffs should be restrained.

19. Countries should produce goods that can be exchanged for raw materials.

20. Dissolution of monopolies, equal prices, and open markets will assure supplies of raw materials.

21. Immigration should be directed to undeveloped countries.

22. Just and humane rules of sea warfare should be revived.

23. Food blockade should be outlawed.[34]

24. The independence of nations should be assured.

25. Small nations should be discouraged from maintaining highly developed armed forces.

26. Small nations should refrain from building economic and military barriers.

27. Consideration should be given to the transfer of minority populations.

28. There can be no lasting peace in Europe with a dismembered Germany.

29. Imperialism must be controlled.

30. The problem of imperialism cannot be solved at the peace table, but international commissions with clear mandates might work.

31. Perhaps some undeveloped areas of the world should be put under international control with equal access to all nations.

32. Disarmament should be a goal.

33. Complete dissolution of all military organization in an enemy nation would be ideal.

34. Disarmament should be immediate among victorious nations.

35. The rate of money spent on arms could be reduced to a minimum and thus permit development in other areas.

36. The sole possessor or possessors of air power could stop anyone from going to war.

37. Disarmament would thus contribute much to recovery.

38. The leaders of nations responsible for the war should be viewed as criminals conspiring to murder.

39. Nations cannot be held in chains.

40. Huge reparations should not be demanded.

41. There cannot be any continuing intergovernmental debt of consequence in either reparations or loans.

42. Victory with vengeance is really defeat.

43. Each nation should agree to refer all disputes to arbitration.

44. The concept of revision of treaties should be built into international law.

45. The number of statesmen involved in peace negotiations should be minimal.

46. There should be three stages of peace-making: (1) a conditioned peace, (2) a "breathing" period, and (3) a period for settlement of long-range problems.

47. Aims of peace should be clear before the end of hostilities.

48. During the recovery period, order must be assured and famine and pestilence must be prevented.

49. The "cold surgery of analysis" must be practiced in achieving a lasting peace.

50. Peace is necessary if civilization is to advance.

The above conclusions represent a combination of pragmatism and idealism, essentially the same kind of combination reflected in Hoover's earlier writings. Some are obvious, and some are naive. As a whole, however, they are the product of two intelligent and humane men whose abundant experiences in world affairs qualify them as analysts of the problems of a lasting peace.

The conclusions, as does the entirety of *The Problems of*

Lasting Peace, emphasize the importance of applying all the lessons of experience in the effort toward peace. After each war and each revolution, men have sought to construct the foundation for a lasting peace; and each time they have failed. Such failure, according to Hoover and Gibson, resulted from the tendency to deal with manifestations rather than fundamental causes. The League of Nations, for example, did not reach the causes of war—six of the seven dynamic forces previously discussed—but flailed ineffectively at superficialities, much like the student council of a public high school. Though Hoover and Gibson had higher hopes for it, the United Nations organization had little more success.

In a short sequel to *The Problems of Lasting Peace*—*The Basis of Lasting Peace* (1945)—Hoover and Gibson trace the differences between the League of Nations and the Dumbarton Oaks proposals that would eventually lead to the United Nations. In this latter work, they reiterate some of the same points discussed in more detail in the former. They list three general methods by which peace can be achieved and attribute one fundamental reason for the League's failure to its attempt "to mix these different and often conflicting methods."[35] These methods are (1) using force to stop aggression, (2) using negotiation and arbitration to settle disputes, and (3) setting in motion those moral, spiritual, political, and social forces which build for peace. "We must," they remind us, "be on our guard against setting up a purely mechanical body without a soul. However ingenious a new world charter may appear on paper it cannot succeed unless it is based upon the great principles of the rights of nations and of individuals." Such a basis they do not see in the Dumbarton Oaks proposals and, therefore, present a list of some fourteen principles that they feel should be included in any new charter. They are, basically, a condensation of the fifty proposals made in *The Problems of Lasting Peace.*

R. M. MacIver, writing in the *New York Times Book Review,* saw this latter book as a good "lead for the momentous conference at San Francisco. Their little volume strikes to the heart of the problem before us, wasting no words and setting the alternatives in the clearest light. It is written so simply that none can misunderstand, and behind its persuasive simplicity there is the statesman's vision."[36]

CHAPTER 8

American Idealism Revisited

""THIS is not a life of Woodrow Wilson," Herbert Hoover tells us in the preface to *The Ordeal of Woodrow Wilson* (1958), but an "analysis of President Wilson's high endeavors, his evangelistic idealism, his successes, his difficulties, the purpose of his compromises, and the consequences of the Treaty of Versailles."[1] There is no doubt that Hoover felt qualified to undertake such an analysis; indeed, he spends a considerable part of the preface describing his engineering background, which took him all over the world and brought him into firsthand contact with many kinds of people and governments and the various governmental appointments he held in the Wilson administration during and after World War I. With that wide experience and with the thirty-nine years of contact with world affairs since the Treaty of Versailles, Hoover expresses the hope that he "can possibly contribute to an understanding of the gigantic tragedy which enveloped Woodrow Wilson and the whole world."[2]

Some may think it strange that a Republican ex-president would write a book on a Democratic president, particularly when the former spoke out so often against foreign entanglements and the latter fought so hard for the League of Nations. On the surface, such a situation may be viewed as one of history's ironies. In a deeper sense, however, there is no irony in the matter. Hoover and Wilson were not that different—at least Hoover did not think so. When he describes Wilson's philosophy, how much like his own it sounds:

His philosophy of American living was based upon free enterprise, both in social and in economic systems. He held that the economic system must be regulated to prevent monopoly and unfair practices. He believed that Federal intervention in the economic or social life of our

127

people was justified only when the task was greater than the states or individuals could perform for themselves.

He yielded with great reluctance to the partial and temporary abandonment of our principles of life during the war, because of the multitude of tasks with which the citizen or the states could not cope. But he often expressed to me the hope that our methods of doing so were such that they could be quickly reversed and free enterprise restored.[3]

Other likenesses come to mind. Both were humanitarians in the truest sense. Both knew great popularity as leaders. Both stumbled in the thicket of politics. Both ended their terms as president under considerable criticism. And, finally, both were misunderstood in their time. If Wilson was ahead of his time, we might well say that Hoover was behind his.

Given his own idealism and moral stance, Hoover's respect for Wilson is not at all surprising. "Three qualities of greatness stood out in Woodrow Wilson," he says. "He was a man of staunch morals. He was more than just an idealist: he was the personification of the heritage of idealism of the American people. He brought spiritual concepts to the peace table. He was a born crusader."[4] Here indeed were two kindred spirits.

I Introduction to Woodrow Wilson

Hoover's first meeting with Woodrow Wilson came in 1915, while Hoover was director of the commission for Relief in Belgium. Hoover was being accused by some of violating the Logan Act, which made it a crime for American citizens to negotiate with foreign governments on international matters. To be sure, he had been in constant negotiation with the governments of Britain, France, and Germany for the protection of the supplies that the commission was sending to Belgium. Hoover felt the matter of significance, feeling that he was merely acting under the auspices of neutral ambassadors and ministers in Europe. Nevertheless, he sailed for the United States and a meeting with President Wilson to discuss the matter. The business portion of the meeting took no more than fifteen minutes as Wilson and Hoover arrived at a publicity strategy to undercut any further criticism of Hoover and the commission. They talked longer, however, on the war, with Wilson asking

Hoover's opinion on the possibilities of American intervention to make peace. "I advised him," writes Hoover, "that the emotional situation among the peoples of the belligerents, if nothing else, made such an effort hopeless at this time."[5]

The impression Hoover leaves us with very early in the book is that Wilson and his chief advisor on peace and war, Colonel Edward M. House, were totally out of touch with the realities of the European situation. They were, he contends, "moving in an idealistic stratosphere far above the earthly ground upon which the war was being fought. It was hard for them to realize that Europe would not recoil from the abyss on the edge of which civilization hung."[6]

Hoover and Wilson next met on January 31, 1917, to discuss a loan for the Relief Commission. The conversation again moved to the war. America was under some pressure to enter the war on the side of the Allies, though Wilson had no intention, according to Hoover, of giving in to that pressure. On February 1, however, Germany declared unlimited submarine war, torpedoing three of the Belgian Relief ships in three days. Still, Hoover had hopes that the Germans could be persuaded to end this unlimited submarine war and advised Wilson that he was sure that the Germans did not want to provoke America into joining the war on the side of the Allies. And he also felt that Wilson "earnestly, and even emotionally, intended to avail himself of every device to keep out, short of national honor."[7]

Both belligerents were badly strained economically, with the Allies being perhaps in the worse condition. Wilson probably hoped that from such strain would come the desire for a negotiated peace. Still, the pressures for joining the Allies were great, and Wilson was finding himself with less and less room for maneuver. Both he and Hoover felt that should America join in defeating Germany, there would be no objective bystander left to mediate a just peace. Frank Cobb of the *New York World* recalled some comments Wilson made one evening:

He said when a war got going it was just war and there weren't two kinds of it. It required illiberalism at home to reinforce the men at the front. We couldn't fight Germany and maintain the ideals of Government that all thinking men shared. He said we would try it but it would be too much for us.

"Once lead this people into war," he said, "and they'll forget there

ever was such a thing as tolerance. To fight you must be brutal and
ruthless, and the spirit of ruthless brutality will enter into the very fibre
of our national life, infecting Congress, the courts, the policeman on the
beat, the man in the street. . . ."

He thought the Constitution would not survive it; that free speech
and the right of assembly would go. He said a nation couldn't put its
strength into a war and keep its head level; it had never been done.

"If there is any alternative, for God's sake, let's take it," he
exclaimed.[8]

II *Wilson and the War*

Whatever the feeling of Wilson and Hoover about entering the
war, they became academic when, on April 16, 1917, the United
States declared war on the Central Powers. Wilson had found the
force of public opinion too strong for him to face the
consequences of not going to war. The question now was how to
organize the nation to contribute to the winning of the war. The
Hoover comments that Wilson was surrounded by able cabinet
members and military leaders to carry out the military aspects of
the war. On the civilian side, however, the need arose for new
agencies to control imports, exports, production, and consumption of everything from war materials to foodstuffs.

Hoover, of course, was never an advocate of governmental
control of the economic sector, but he was realist enough at this
point to recognize the need for governmental activities that
were strange in American life—so strange in fact that "Congress
was tardy, fearful and often inadequate in conferring the powers
upon the President which were vital to enable the civilian
agencies to contribute their part in winning the war."[9] Wilson
himself sought to defuse the argument that such powers were
dictatorial by having them administered by boards, commissions,
or committees. Hoover warned him that such a strategy would
prove, as it had earlier for the Allies, inefficient and clumsy.
Here was one occasion when Hoover, so ardent a supporter of
representative government, showed another dimension—that of
the engineer-administrator. He convinced Wilson that, at least as
far as his position as head of the Food Administration was
concerned, he should be given the title "Administrator," which
would not connote dictatorship, but which would still centralize
power in a single executive—"the basic concept of organization

of our Government and our business world ever since the foundation of the Republic."[10] For Hoover, such a view presented no paradox.

Hoover credits Wilson with making appointments irrespective of political faiths of well-qualified men to direct the needed organizations. The picture he presents is that of a smoothly functioning machine—exporting three times as much food as usual, raising armies of 3 million men, and expanding an already strong navy. Moreover, Wilson's religious and moral upbringing "expressed itself in a zeal for financial integrity which characterized the conduct of a war practically without corruption."[11] Various persons may have criticized Wilson's management of the war, but Hoover presents him as a talented administrator who knew how to delegate work and how to evaluate problems quickly.[12]

Near the end of the war, Wilson made an appeal for the election of a Democratic Congress, an appeal that shocked Hoover. In a speech of October 24, 1918, Wilson said,

The return of a Republican majority to either House of the Congress would, moreover, certainly be interpreted on the other side of the water as a repudiation of my leadership. Spokesmen of the Republican Party are urging you to elect a Republican Congress in order to back up and support the President, but even if they should in this way impose upon some credulous voters on this side of the water, they would impose on no one on the other side. It is well understood there as well as here that the Republican leaders desire not so much to support the President as to control him.[13]

Hoover finds such an attack on the Republicans as not only an unwarranted act, but also as a mystery—a mystery lying "in the identify of the politicians who pushed Mr. Wilson into an action so entirely foreign to his nature and his previous nonpartisan conduct of war affairs."[14] Whatever he felt, Hoover nevertheless supported Wilson in his appeal for a Democratic Congress, an act of loyalty that deeply touched Wilson, who wrote to Hoover that "I want you to know not only how proud I am to have your endorsement and your backing given in such generous fashion, but also what serious importance I attach to it, for I have learned to value your judgment and have the greatest trust in all your moral reactions. I thank you from the bottom of my heart."[15]

Hoover's fellow Republicans, on the other hand, were not so pleased, as Hoover noted in his *Memoirs:* "My only participation in politics during the war got me in some hot water."[16] Hoover's support, however, did no good, or at least not enough good; and the Democrats lost both houses of Congress in the November elections. "Subsequent events," says Hoover, "show that the President's influence at Paris and his influence with the Senate to obtain ratification of the peace were definitely damaged."[17]

III   *New World Ideals of Peace*

Woodrow Wilson, realizing that negotiating a peace following the war could be even more difficult and far-reaching than gaining the military victory, began defining his version of the basis for peace as early as April 1917, when he pointed out that, regardless of the actions of the German government, America had no quarrel with the German people. Peace could only be achieved by a concert of free peoples and not by motives of self-interest. America, he said, wanted "no conquest, no dominion. We seek no indemnities for ourselves, no material compensation for the sacrifices we shall freely make."[18]

Between January and December of 1918, Wilson made four major addresses in which he presented a number of principles for peace.[19] These principles ultimately totaled thirty-eight, but the essence of them is found in the first "Fourteen Points," which he laid down in the first of the four addresses—an address to Congress on January 8, 1918:

I.—Open covenants of peace, openly arrived at, after which there shall be no private international understandings of any kind but diplomacy shall proceed always frankly and in the public view.

II.—Absolute freedom of navigation upon the seas, outside territorial waters, alike in peace and in war, except as the seas may be closed in whole or in part by international action for the enforcement of international covenants.

III.—The removal, so far as possible, of all economic barriers and the establishment of an equality of trade conditions among all the nations consenting to the peace and associating themselves for its maintenance.

IV.—Adequate guarantees given and taken that national armaments will be reduced to the lowest point consistent with domestic safety.

V.—Free, open-minded, and absolutely impartial adjustment of all colonial claims, based upon a strict observance of the principle that in determining all such questions of sovereignty the interests of the populations concerned must have equal weight with the equitable claims of the Government whose title is to be determined.

VI.—The evacuation of all Russian territory and such a settlement of all questions affecting Russia as will secure the best and freest cooperation of the other nations of the world in obtaining for her an unhampered and unembarrassed opportunity for the independent determination of her own political development and national policy and assure her of a sincere welcome into the society of free nations under institutions of her own choosing; and, more than a welcome, assistance also of every kind that she may need and may herself desire. The treatment accorded Russia by her sister nations in the months to come will be the acid test of their good will, of their comprehension of her needs as distinguished from their own interests, and of their intelligent and unselfish sympathy.

VII.—Belgium, the whole world will agree, must be evacuated and restored, without any attempt to limit the soveriegnty which she enjoys in common with all other free nations. No other single act will serve as this will serve to restore confidence among the nations in the laws which they have themselves set and determined for the government of their relations with one another. Without this healing act the whole structure and validity of international law is forever impaired.

VIII.—All French territory should be freed and the invaded portions restored, and the wrong done to France by Prussia in 1871 in the matter of Alsace-Lorraine, which has unsettled the peace of the world for nearly fifty years, should be righted, in order that peace may once more be made secure in the interest of all.

IX.—A readjustment of the frontiers of Italy should be effected along clearly recognizable lines of nationality.

X.—The peoples of Austria-Hungary, whose place among the nations we wish to see safeguarded and assured, should be accorded the freest opportunity of autonomous development.

XI.—Rumania, Serbia, and Montenegro should be evacuated; occupied territories restored; Serbia accorded free and secure access to the sea; and the relations of the several Balkan States to one another determined by friendly counsel along historically established lines of allegiance and nationality; and international guarantees of the political and economic independence and territorial integrity of the several Balkan States should be entered into.

XII.—The Turkish portions of the present Ottoman Empire should be assured a secure sovereignty, but the other nationalities which are now under Turkish rule should be assured an undoubted security of life and an absolutely unmolested opportunity of autonomous development, and the Dardanelles should be permanently opened as a free passage to the ships and commerce of all nations under international guarantees.

XIII.—An independent Polish State should be erected which should include the territories inhabited by indisputably Polish populations, which should be assured a free and secure access to the sea, and whose political and economic independence and territorial integrity should be guaranteed by international covenant.

XIV.—A general association of nations must be formed under specific covenants for the purpose of affording mutual guarantees of political independence and territorial integrity to great and small states alike.[20]

When Germany and Austria-Hungary finally sought an armistice, they turned to Wilson and his Fourteen Points as bases of negotiation. The latter was quite willing to accept the responsibility of a leading role in any negotiations, for he knew as well as the Central Powers did that the best chance for a just peace lay in mitigating the forces of hatred and revenge that undoubtedly burned in the minds and hearts of the Allies. Wilson, then, at once took control of the negotiations, with, as Hoover outlines, a three-fold purpose: "First, to assure before peace negotiations the withdrawal of enemy troops from occupied territory and the reduction of the strength of the enemy armies to impotence. Second, to establish securely the 'Fourteen Points and the subsequent addresses' as a basis for peace for Germany and the other enemy states. Third, and of equal or greater importance as we shall see in the next chapter, to secure agreement from the Allies that they, too, would adhere to the 'Fourteen Points and the subsequent addresses' as the basis of peace."[21]

Hoover goes on to lay out day by day the events that occurred as armistice negotiations were carried on between September 16, 1918, when the Austro-Hungarian government requested a conference to consider an armistice, to November 11, 1918, when an armistice was finally concluded with the Germans. These events, in his mind, represent "the greatest drama of intellectual leadership in all history."[22]

Following Austria-Hungary's overture to Wilson, events unfolded rapidly: Bulgaria surrendered; Prince Max of Baden succeeded to the German chancellorship; and Germany and Austria-Hungary requested an armistice—all in less than one month. While the Allied governments were demanding not only withdrawal on the part of the Central Powers from occupied territory, but also an immediate disarmament, Hoover pictures

Wilson as moving very deliberately in facing questions which he felt needed a step-by-step approach. Once the Germans and Austro-Hungarians agreed to withdraw their troops, then Wilson pushed for a reduction in armaments. Germany was evasive regarding disarmament, but Wilson prevailed. Both Germany and Austria-Hungary agreed to an armistice and to peace negotiations.

Above all, Wilson wanted to assure an armistice that was as moderate and reasonable as possible under the circumstances, because he was deeply concerned that too severe an armistice would preclude a genuine peace settlement. Hoover credits his courage and skill with turning "the German request for an armistice during which to negotiate the peace with their armies still standing into a complete surrender, and more, he had fully established his 'basis of peace' with them."[23]

Getting the Germans and the Austro-Hungarians to agree to withdraw from occupied territories and to demobilize their troops as a basis for peace negotiations was one thing; getting the Allies to accept that basis was another. Britain's Lloyd George, for example, balked on Point Two, which dealt with complete freedom of the seas, because it took away the power of blockade—a power England held to be essential to her survival. The idea of the League of Nations was also in some trouble. Colonel House, who was representing Wilson, called the president, suggesting that "you begin to gently shut down upon money, food and raw material."[24] Wilson held firm on his Fourteen Points, though he agreed that freedom of the seas should be subject to negotiation, and the Allies accepted them as a basis for peace negotiations on November 4. Hoover describes Wilson's accomplishment as "one of the most monumental feats of international action of any statesman of history. Singlehanded he had maneuvered the Germans from their island of safety where they might have negotiated with their armies still standing, into almost complete surrender. And equally vital, he had won Allied agreement to the basis of peace laid down in his Fourteen Points. . . . It was a vast triumph for Woodrow Wilson and a war-weary mankind."[25]

The triumph that Hoover credits to Wilson was the first step in the latter's plan for peace negotiations that were attended by negotiators rather than by victors and defeated—to produce, in Hofstadter's words, "not simply 'a peace without victory,' but a victory to be followed by an unvictorious peace."[26] For such to happen, it was essential that the United States play a disinterested role, careful not to appear to be siding with the enemy and just as careful not to allow the Allies to sow the seeds of a future war through vengeful and vindictive demands upon Germany. Not an easy task.

Wilson, in what Hoover depicts as "one of the pivotal acts of the titanic world drama,"[27] decided to go to Europe to personally head the American peace delegation. The president had advice both pro and con regarding his going to Europe, but in the end it was, according to Hoover, Wilson's own decision. As we have seen earlier, Hoover was opposed to Wilson's idea to involve himself directly in the negotiations: "From my own experience, I was convinced that Mr. Wilson's New World idealism would clash seriously with the Old World concepts of the Allied statesmen, and I feared that the President's dominant voice in creating world opinion would be stilled if he became involved in the inevitable restraints of personal negotiation."[28] More than that, Wilson would lose the power that his position in Washington provided, a position from which he had the ear of the world. Hoover quotes Frank I. Cobb, one of Colonel House's assistants in Paris: "The President, if he is to win this great battle for human freedom, must fight on his own ground and his own ground is Washington. Diplomatic Europe is all enemy soil for him. He cannot make a successful appeal to the people of the world here. The official surroundings are all unfavorable. The means of minimizing its effect are all under the control of those who are opposed to him. One of his strongest weapons in his conflict is the very mystery and uncertainty that attach to him while he remains in Washington."[29]

Wilson, however, felt that remaining in Washington would keep him too far away from, and too uninformed about, what was happening at the peace table. "It was inevitable," said his private secretary, Charles Swem, "that he [Wilson] himself should go to the Peace Conference. Every habit of thought bound him, every dictate of principle to which he responded, every circumstance of the time, made it impossible for him to be absent. . . . He had striven to win the war that he might have a part in the settlement that followed. . . ."[30] Even the knowledge that neither Clemenceau nor Lloyd George was receptive to his direct participation in the negotiations could not shake Wilson's determination to sail for Europe.

Wilson arrived in Paris on December 14, 1918. Hoover talked with him two days later, cautioning him regarding "the shapes of evil inherent in the Old World system."[31] The warning at the time made little impression on the president, who was no doubt basking in the fervent reception the people of Europe were giving him. Three months later, however, he remarked wearily to Hoover that the latter's warning had been accurate enough.

Hoover describes the stage upon which Woodrow Wilson was to play his role as peacemaker as one of turmoil—peopled by protagonists and antagonists motivated by long-standing rivalries and conflicts. For them, peace negotiations were simply another kind of war, no less significant than military war. As a character in this drama, Wilson was not welcome. "With his flaming banner of the 'Fourteen Points and the subsequent address,' his eloquence about self-determination, his denunciations of annexations. . .Mr. Wilson was a menacing intruder in the concepts of British, French, and Italian statesmen and a threat to their secret treaties dividing all Europe. . . ."[32]

Wilson's program of self-determination, free trade, and a League of Nations came into direct conflict with "empire," whose roots were centuries deep in Europe and whose concepts the victorious nations were not about to give up without a struggle. When he spoke in Manchester, England, on December 30, 1918, against the balance of power concept and military alliances as roots of evil in the Old World, Clemenceau of France responded one day later before the French Chamber of Deputies, "There is an old system of alliances called the 'balance of power.' It seems to be condemned nowadays, but if such a balance had preceded the war, if England, the United States, France, and Italy had agreed, say, that whoever attacked one of them attacked the whole world, the war would not have occurred. This system of alliances, which I do not renounce, will be my guiding thought at the Peace Conference if your confidence sends me there."[33] He received, according to Hoover, a three-to-one vote of confidence following his speech.

Hoover credits Wilson the historian as being no doubt familiar with the age-old forces operative in European politics, but he does not see Wilson the president as aware of the dynamism of those forces. Indeed, his popular reception by the people in Europe seems to confirm in his mind that there was a new and constructive spirit of righteousness and idealism rising from the ashes of the war.

In nurturing this new spirit he so much wanted to bear fruit, Wilson faced a number of obstacles in addition to those mentioned above. The American people, for example, though far from Europe geographically, were not free of the emotions of hate and vengeance in their feelings toward the Germans. Wilson was faced, as was Hoover, with the charge from his own countrymen of being pro-German. His own Fourteen Points— particularly the idea of self-determination—fired the spirit of nationalism among the newly created states of Eastern Europe, bringing exaggerated demands for territory. Under the American system of the separation of powers, Wilson, unlike the European prime ministers, carried no authority to bind his government. The American peace delegation was lacking in the skill and experience of diplomacy needed to counter that which they faced from their European counterparts. They were, says Hoover, "mostly amateurs and college professors."[34] And, too, Wilson found himself in a maze of secret treaties and agreements entered into by the Allies before America entered the war. Hoover sums up his own view of the problems faced by Wilson by saying that "in the larger sense, the forces which weakened the President's influence at Paris were far deeper than the intrigues or the secret agreements between Allied statesmen. Here was the collision of civilizations that had grown centuries apart. Here the idealism of the Western World was in clash with the racial mores and the grim determination of many nations at the peace table to have revenge, reparations and territorial spoils. At the Peace Conference the ordeal of Woodrow Wilson began and the forces inherent in the Old World took over the control of human fate."[35]

IV   *Administrative Ordeal*

In the midst of the drama of the peace negotiations, it is easy to overlook the vast amount of administrative detail that was involved. Hoover points to a multitude of inter-Allied councils, committees, or boards for administrative coordination that evolved during the course of the war—most of which continued during the peace conference. He at one time during the negotiations counted more than sixty such bodies, himself a member of twenty and chairman of six.

As mentioned earlier, Hoover recommended to Wilson the formation of an American economic council to coordinate economic policies during the negotiations. Hoover served on the council, called the President's Committee of Economic Advisors. "Next to the Peace Conference itself," Hoover says, "the most important American activity during the peacemaking and for some time afterward was the Relief and Reconstruction of Europe, under my direction."[36] He pictures Wilson as very much concerned with this aspect of American activities at Versailles, primarily because it touched his humane spirit, as well as having significant political implications.

One of the first problems that faced Wilson and Hoover in this area was the fear among European leaders that the United States would attempt to use its resources as a lever to force them into accepting Wilson's peace plan. Because of that fear, they wanted all relief and reconstruction conducted solely in the name of the Allied and Associated Powers. Not only was it a matter of prestige, it was also a very practical matter of gaining a position from which to exert political pressure on the many smaller nations involved in the Peace Conference. Such a situation was repugnant to both Wilson and Hoover—Hoover seeing it as one more example of the fundamental conflict between Old and New World concepts. The Allies saw their recovery from the war hinging "not only on maintaining 'empire' but expanding it and increasing their power and prestige to do so. Their motive was empire first, and their bureaucracies thought only in such terms."[37]

Hoover's own impatience with bureaucratic haggling is made clear when he says that he decided that Wilson could get further in the upper echelons than he himself could with bureaucrats; and, consequently, he went ahead with relief for the hungry.

Wilson did get further with the prime ministers, and his plan for relief and reconstruction was finally accepted. Hoover had originally wanted to return to America and his professional career as soon as the organization for relief and reconstruction was completed, but Wilson bluntly stated, "You cannot leave me with this worry in the hands of some new man and expect me to make peace as well."[38] So Hoover accepted the appointment of director general of the renamed American Relief Administration.

Hoover goes on to list many of the obstacles that Wilson was forced to deal with personally regarding the American Relief Administration. Most of the emphasis in this part of the book, however, is on Hoover's activities, with Wilson mentioned only as having agreed to this plan or taking that advice as it was suggested or offered by Hoover. In fact, we are inclined to forget for awhile at least that this is a book on Wilson and not on Hoover. Nevertheless, the American Relief Administration became known to hundreds of millions of people all over Europe for its efforts in combating starvation.

Another problem facing Wilson, which, according to Hoover, drained his vitality, was that of Communist activity in spreading revolution over Central and Eastern Europe. "Communist Russia," he writes, "was a specter which wandered into the Peace Conference almost daily."[39] Nor did the Big Four (Wilson, Clemenceau, Lloyd George, and Orlando) know how to deal with it. The British and French advocated a general attack on Russia. Wilson, however, was strongly opposed to any such action, saying, "It would be fatal to be led further into the Russian chaos."[40] Hoover, too, as much as he feared and detested communism, advised against participating in any armed intervention in Russian affairs. The plan he recommended to Wilson was that a neutral person of international reputation be supported in setting up a relief commission to aid the Russian people, thus buying time "to determine whether or not this whole system [communism] is a world danger, and whether the Russian people will not themselves swing back to moderation and themselves bankrupt these ideas."[41]

Wilson accepted Hoover's plan, as did the other Allied leaders, and the Norwegian explorer Fridtjof Nansen was asked to head the relief organization. The Russians were willing to accept the relief, but they were not willing to give up fighting until they had won their objectives. Although Hoover was still hopeful that some arrangements could be made, the French denounced the entire effort, bringing it to an end.

The Baltic states of Finland, Estonia, Latvia, and Lithuania were struggling for their survival as independent nations. Having thrown off the yoke of Czarist Russia, they were now striving to stay out of the clutches of Communist Russia. Hoover, with Wilson's backing, was instrumental in aiding these small countries through providing food supplies to sustain them in their determination to be nations in their own right. While their democratic ambitions were not, except in Finland, fully realized in the ensuing years, still they were independent nations until 1940, when Russia seized Latvia, Estonia, and Lithuania and a part of Finland. "The restoration of these states to Western civilization," says Hoover, "may come again some day. Races whose mores have survived a thousand years of foreign oppression do not easily perish."[42]

Article XXI of the armistice agreement provided for the maintenance of the Allied blockade on the former enemy nations, ostensibly to maintain political control of the Continent until the final peace arrangements were made. Wilson and the American peace delegation, says Hoover, "considered a rigid blockade utter folly because it created unemployment, prevented economic recovery and fertilized Communism."[43] We have seen earlier the strong views Hoover held against this blockade. Wilson was able to get the Allies to agree to the provisioning of Germany during the Armistice, and Hoover prepared a plan for that provisioning.

On December 31, however, the Allied blockade authorities reversed their decision and reinstituted a tight blockade on all Europe that lasted four months. "It was," writes Hoover, "a crime in statesmanship against civilization as a whole. It sowed dragon's teeth of war which two decades later again enveloped most of mankind. But no one who reads the documents and records of the time will ever charge that crime against President Wilson and America. Yet we in the United States have had to suffer from this infection of revenge and bitterness which for a generation poisoned international life."[44]

While much of what Hoover discusses in this section of *The Ordeal of Woodrow Wilson* relates to Wilson only peripherally, it does provide more insight into Hoover's own thinking. He describes the many conferences held and quotes from various letters and memoranda regarding his efforts to get food supplies through to the German people and emphasizes the negative effects the continuation of the blockade had on German

attitudes for years afterward. He places it in the context of the
desire for vengeance on the part of the Allies, with America the
only nation trying to act in a truly humanitarian way.

V   The League of Nations

Whatever other burdens Woodrow Wilson faced during this
period, his primary challenge was to work toward a just and
lasting peace. Hoover divides this challenge into two parts: (1)
establishing the League of Nations and (2) framing the treaty
with Germany. The first of the two was really his primary goal,
because through the league he felt sure that any faults arising in
the treaty could be worked out to the satisfaction of all.

Wilson's first public reference to his dream of a league of
nations came on May 27, 1916, when he said that ". . .the
nations of the world must in some way band themselves together
to see that right prevails as against any sort of selfish
aggression;. . .I am sure that I speak the mind and wish of the
people of America when I say that the United States is willing to
become a partner in any feasible association of nations formed in
order to realize these objects and make them secure against
violation."[45]

Both Wilson and the British came to Paris with drafts of
constitutions for a league of nations. The first step was to obtain
an acceptance from the peace conference of the principle of the
league and that it should be an integral part of any ensuing peace
treaty. Wilson, according to Hoover, spoke eloquently in behalf
of the league, emphasizing "that when it is known. . .that we
have adopted the principle of the League of Nations and mean to
work out that principle in effective action, we shall by that single
thing have lifted a great part of the load of anxiety from the
hearts of men everywhere. . . ."[46] The principle of the league
was accepted in plenary session on January 25, 1919, and a
special committee, with Wilson as chairman, was appointed to
draft the covenant.

A draft was submitted to, and accepted by, a plenary session of
the delegates on February 14, 1919. Wilson's speech accompanying the draft to the delegates showed the dimensions with
which he perceived the league. He saw it as going beyond
merely securing peace; it would provide the basis for international cooperation on any matter. Describing it as both a

practical and humane document, he went on to say, "There is a pulse of sympathy in it. There is a compulsion of conscience throughout it. It is practical, and yet it is intended to purify, to rectify, to elevate. . . ."[47]

The draft was not without its critics, either at the peace conference or in the United States Senate. The day after the plenary session accepted the league covenant, Wilson left for America to explain it to the American public and to the Senate Foreign Relations Committee and the House Foreign Relations Committee. A number of the Republican members of the committees found fault with the league covenant because it did not recognize the Monroe Doctrine; it failed to provide specifically that the league would not interfere in domestic affairs; it did not state the right of a nation to withdraw; and it presented a threat to the right of Congress to make peace and war. Moreover, some thirty-seven Republican members of the Senate signed a resolution proposing that the league covenant not be accepted by the United States. Because of imminent adjournment, this resolution was never acted upon.

Hoover traces the bitterness among these senators, many of whom had supported Wilson during the war, to his partisan statement against Republicans in the congressional campaign four months earlier. When he returned to Europe on March 14, 1919, however, Wilson faced even more significant problems in his efforts to bring life to the League.

Wilson had left Europe for his short visit back to the United States with such esteem and such good wishes for his return that, according to Hoover, "it seemed at the time of his departure for New York that he had only to come back for a few weeks to this friendly atmosphere and complete a few remaining items to reach his final triumph."[48] During his absence, however, the Allies began to make new demands regarding territorial acquisition, prompting Wilson to comment during the return voyage "that these men [Lloyd George and Clemenceau] have agreed on a definite programme. Apparently they are determined to get everything out of Germany they can, now that she is helpless."[49]

Wilson was unequivocally opposed to such a "game of grab," maintaining his view that any lasting peace would have to be a just peace to the defeated nations. So strong were his feelings on this point that he privately expressed a threat to return home and eventually conclude a separate peace. This, however, was never a serious consideration for Wilson; but it does show his impatience with Allied machinations. Once back in Paris, Wilson entered into direct and secret negotiations with the Allied prime ministers to try to give new impetus to his ideas for peace. "Unfortunately," says Hoover, "by the secrecy of these discussions the President had disarmed himself of his greatest weapon—appeal to the great world public that regarded him as the rightful leader of the crusade for the emancipation of mankind."[50]

Lloyd George issued a memorandum on March 25 that called for a treaty of moderation with Germany and an effort to unite in all states the various national groups. This latter principle was aimed at stopping annexation moves by the newly created Eastern European states of the territory of other national groups. Moreover, Lloyd George recommended early admission of Germany to the league. Clemenceau's response to this memorandum was a strong statement for the inclusion of German minorities among smaller states and the reduction of Germany to a point where she could pose no military threat to France.

Clemenceau, in Hoover's view,

. . .personified all the emotions and sufferings of the French people. Twice in his lifetime he had witnessed German hobnailed boots on French soil. Constantly in his mind's eye were German brutalities, destroyed French homes, the dead and injured, the widows and orphans. In this last aggression the Germans had left behind about 1,400,000 French dead and 740,000 seriously wounded and they had taken 400,000 French prisoners. The Old Tiger had no confidence that Germany had gone through any spiritual transformation either by defeat or by the Reichstag revolution against the Kaiser and the militarist group. Nor did he have any faith in President Wilson or his "Fourteen Points, and the subsequent addresses."[51]

In such an atmosphere, Woodrow Wilson became ill and had to retire from the arena of peace negotiations. During his absence, the Allied negotiators continued in their efforts to shape a treaty to their liking; and when, upon regaining some of his strength, Wilson asked to be brought up to date on matters, what he heard brought disappointment and resignation. Hoover quotes Mrs. Wilson's recollection of that time:

More days of tense anxiety. Getting better, the President insisted on knowing what had gone forward while he had been incapacitated. Alas, his absence had been taken advantage of again. The news that came to him was so grave we trembled for the effect on him. But the spirit was stronger than the flesh, and instead of causing a relapse it stiffened his will. Silently I sat beside his bed, knowing that he was formulating his course. At length he said: "I can never sign a Treaty made on these lines, and if all the rest of the delegates have determined on this, I will not be a party to it. If I have lost my fight, which I would not have done had I been on my feet, I will retire in good order; so we will go home. Call Grayson for me, please."[52]

Hoover's advice to Wilson at this time was to present the Allies with the ultimatum that, unless they were to come nearer to the American position, the United States would indeed withdraw from the negotiations and pursue a separate peace with Germany. Others advised Wilson that withdrawing from the talks would place the responsibility of their failure upon his shoulders and that he should remain to the very end, demanding the acceptance of his principles. Hoover's point was that the Allies would in the end accept Wilson's points in order not to lose American financial support. Wilson decided to give it another try and resumed conferences with Lloyd George, Clemenceau, and Orlando.

VI   *Ordeal of Compromise*

When negotiations resumed, Italy renewed claims for Fiume, an Adriatic port now part of Yugoslavia, and for a larger share of Dalmatia, arguing that such was agreed to among Britain, France, and Italy in 1915.[53] Wilson, of course, saw this demand as a blatant violation of his principles and attempted to persuade Orlando to withdraw it. Wilson's attempt failed, and on April 25, 1919, Italy withdrew from the peace conference. In Italy, says Hoover, "there were many fiery speeches denouncing the President. The Italian people tore down their tributes to Mr. Wilson and burned him in effigy."[54]

Hoover pictures Wilson during this period of the negotiations as a man in deep troubles. The Japanese, for example, seeing the difficulty the Italian withdrawal was causing Wilson, quickly made demands for rights in Shantung Province in China, or they

too would withdraw.[55] Such pressures, along with the invitation
to the Germans to be in Paris on April 28 to receive peace terms,
forced Wilson into compromises that he certainly would rather
not have made, but which he felt essential in order to save the
League of Nations.

Wilson's first compromise, although Hoover and a number of
other aides strongly advised him against it, was to yield to the
Japanese demand for rights in Shantung Province. Wilson did
seek unsuccessfully to extract a written agreement from the
Japanese that they would eventually relinquish those rights.

A number of compromises concerned French demands for the
virtual dismemberment of Germany. The first steps in this
dismemberment, to which Wilson agreed, involved the prohibition of any joining together of Germany and Austria; the
transferring control of 2 million Sudeten Germans from Austria
to Czechoslovakia; transferring control of 1.5 million Austro-
Germans from Austria to Italy; establishing the Polish Corridor
to the Baltic; and the annexation of Upper Silesia by Poland, by
which 1.5 million Germans came under Polish control. The
French also wanted the Rhineland separated from Germany (as
an independent state), but Wilson would go only so far as to allow
Allied occupation of that area for fifteen years.

One of the more dramatic exchanges between Wilson and
Clemenceau occurred, according to Hoover, when the French
claimed the Saar, a small but rich German coal district. He
quotes from Colonel House's description of that exchange:

. . .The President told Clemenceau that the French were bringing up
territorial questions that had nothing to do with the war aims of
anybody, and that no one had heard of their intention to annex the Saar
Valley until after the Armistice had been signed. Clemenceau grew
angry at this and said that the President favored the Germans. The
President replied that such a statement was untrue and that
Clemenceau knew that it was.

Clemenceau then stated that if they did not receive the Saar Valley,
he would not sign the Treaty of Peace. To this the President replied,
"Then if France does not get what she wishes, she will refuse to act
with us. In that event do you wish me to return home?" Clemenceau
answered, "I do not wish you to go home, but I intend to do so myself,"
and in a moment he left the house.[56]

The compromise finally worked out on the Saar gave control

of the mines to the League of Nations for a period of fifteen years, during which time the French were to receive the entire coal output.

Referring to Clemenceau as the "Old Tiger," Hoover lists a number of other demands made by the French and the compromises Wilson was forced to make in response to those demands: a military alliance among France, Britain, and the United States, to which Wilson agreed (an obvious violation of Wilson's basis for peace); unfixed sum of reparations to be paid by Germany; guilt confession by the German people as a whole; annexation of mandated territories to the Allies (Britain, France, Italy, and Japan)[57]; and the reinstitution of the blockade should Germany not sign the Treaty.

Wilson, through the above compromises, was successful in winning agreement from the Allies to the covenant of the League of Nations. Hoover, however, quickly points out that the focal point of the peace conference was not the league but the treaty itself—because through the treaty the entire structure of Europe was to be rebuilt. The treaty contained 75,000 words, only 4,000 of which dealt with the league covenant.

VII   A *Treaty of Retribution*

Again in this book—and in more detail than in either *The Problems of Lasting Peace* or his *Memoirs*—Hoover displays his own negative reaction to the Treaty of Versailles:

I certainly had no admiration for the conduct of the German militarists. But if the world was to have peace, it had, in my mind, to choose one of two alternatives: to reduce Germany to such poverty and political degradation that initiative and genius would be extinguished; or to give her terms that would permit the new representative government under President Ebert to live with the hope that free government might develop the nation as a peaceful member of the family of mankind. If this were not done, there would come either a return of the sullen militarists or the already infectious Communists—both with aggression in their souls.

I was convinced that the terms set up in this draft of the Treaty would degrade all Europe and that peace for the long run could not be built on these foundations. I believed the Treaty contained the seeds of another war. It seemed to me that the economic provisions alone would pull down the whole Continent and, in the end, injure the United States.[58]

Hoover recalls sitting for hours with a number of his colleagues poring over the treaty—shocked at how far removed it was from Wilson's original basis for peace, upon which the Germans had surrendered. The Germans, too, were shocked and repeatedly pointed out how far removed the treaty was from Wilson's Fourteen Points.

While Clemenceau remained adamant in his stance that the treaty be accepted as it was, the British came to favor making some concessions in the harshness of its conditions. Hoover and others urged Wilson to take advantage of this British willingness to compromise, but Wilson demurred, stating that a hard treaty was needed and that as soon as Germany was admitted to the League of Nations, all problems would be solved. Moreover, as he told Hoover later, "Lloyd George will not stand up against Clemenceau despite what he says."[59] To Wilson's credit, he did call upon Lloyd George, advising him that the American position was to accept any amendments that the British would accept— but since "he [Wilson] had in the first place opposed these very inclusions in the Treaty, which Lloyd George now proposed to amend, and as the British Prime Minister had sided with Clemenceau, he insisted that Lloyd George first obtain Clemenceau's agreement."[60]

Clemenceau could not be budged, and Wilson fell back to his position that "the men and forces which dominated Europe could not be surmounted at this time, that the world must be saved from chaos by signing the Treaty and that there was hope that its wrongs could be cured in time by the League."[61] After some delay and a change of government, the Germans signed the treaty and the world was once more at peace.

Despite his own unhappiness with the treaty, Hoover praises the great gains for mankind that Woodrow Wilson achieved through his steadfast leadership and willing sacrifices. The League of Nations, whatever its weaknesses, was the world's first effort at a systematic organization of nations to maintain peace. Beyond that, Hoover sees Wilson as having contributed significantly to the political independence and self-determination of many of the world's peoples. "History should," says Hoover of Wilson, "record the role of his great proclamations in the quest for freedom, and the many acknowledgments from people who attained it."[62]

VIII   *Last Crusade*

Wilson left Europe on June 28, 1918, to launch his crusade for Senate ratification of the Treaty of Versailles. Hoover returned two months later. The two had no opportunity to talk at length for over two years, though they were both vitally concerned with the ratification of the treaty.

The greatest opposition Wilson faced focused on Article X of the covenant of the league—an article which guaranteed the borders of all thirty-two signatories to the League. To Wilson, this article was the backbone of the league. To remove it would turn the league into little more than a debating society. Hoover, on the other hand, felt that the league would be more effective without Article X, primarily because he saw the guaranteeing of so many borders a very difficult, if not impossible, task. Despite this difference of views, Hoover defended the league as the one hope for correcting the faults of the treaty.

Wilson carried his argument for ratification to the nation, delivering forty speeches in twenty-seven cities between Washington and the Pacific coast. Hoover describes these speeches as "moving and impressive." They were delivered extemporaneously and attempted to explain the various compromises made to insure final acceptance of the treaty. The strain of such an effort was too much for Wilson, and on September 25, 1919, he suffered a stroke. His crusade was over.

Hoover attempts to clear up some of the mystery of Wilson's illness and the effect it had upon the functioning of the government. As in most cases with a president's illness, the exact seriousness of Wilson's was not made public until long afterward; but, drawing on quotations from a number of sources, including Mrs. Wilson, and combining them with his own knowledge of the situation, Hoover presents a poignant picture of a president unable physically to carry on his duties, yet unwilling spiritually to allow his ideals to be distorted through dishonorable compromise. He could not, for example, accept the fourteen amendments to the league covenant and the treaty that the Senate Foreign Relations Committee proposed.

The Senate voted on November 19, 1919, and defeated ratification by seven votes of the necessary two-thirds of the Senators present. Speaking on numerous occasions, Hoover himself carried on a defense of the covenant and the treaty in Wilson's behalf. But again on March 19, 1920, the Senate defeated ratification by the same margin. Hoover's estimation of the situation is brief and pointed: "The President had accepted far more of 'the lesser evils' at Paris than were implied in the reservations. But Mr. Wilson was completely isolated from the political currents in motion and from those personal contacts essential for evolving successful cooperation with the Senate. He was a very ill man. While his mind may have been clear in the opinion of those around him, his lack of contact with the people and their leaders separated him from the reality of which sound compromises are made."[63]

Wilson, of course, was unable to take an active part in the campaign of 1920, which pitted Democrat James Cox of Ohio against Republican Warren Harding. The Democratic platform gave full support to Wilson, the league, and the treaty. The Republican platform, writes Hoover, "attacked the League but contained words on the desirability of 'an agreement among nations to preserve the peace of the world.' It was a weak attempt at a straddle."[64]

Whatever his views of their platform, Hoover did renew his ties with the Republicans, joining a committee headed by former President William Taft that had been expressing support for the league and the treaty. With the other members of this committee, Hoover traversed the country speaking in behalf of Wilson's dream. Events in Europe, however, worked to diminish the American people's support of the league and the treaty: French armies occupied Frankfurt; the British and French rejected the demands of Arab mandates for independence; small wars continued in Eastern Europe; and armaments were increased by virtually every European country. Moreover, there was little expression of appreciation from Europe for American aid to Europe.

The climate for ratification continued to deteriorate after Harding's election, until the United States finally negotiated separate treaties with Germany and the other Central Powers. All that Wilson had dreamed of and worked for was dead—killed by the forces of international diplomacy and domestic bitterness.

In just over two years, Woodrow Wilson, too, was dead. The irony of his ordeal was not lost on Hoover:

For a moment at the time of the Armistice, Mr. Wilson rose to intellectual domination of most of the civilized world. With his courage and eloquence, he carried a message of hope for the independence of nations, the freedom of men and lasting peace. Never since his time has any man risen to the political and spiritual heights that came to him. His proclaimed principles of self-government and independence aided the spread of freedom to twenty-two races at the time of the Armistice.

But he was to find that his was a struggle between the concepts of the New and Old Worlds. European statesmen were dominated by the forces of hate and revenge of their peoples for grievous wrongs; by the economic prostration of their peoples; and by the ancient system of imperial spoils. Mr. Wilson was forced to compromise with their demands in order to save the League, confident that it would in time right the wrongs that had been done.[65]

IX   *Whose Story?*

As readers of *The Ordeal of Woodrow Wilson* we may understandably wonder on occasion whether we are reading about Woodrow Wilson or about Herbert Hoover. This is not to say that Hoover does not present a detailed picture of Wilson during and after the peace conference, for certainly Hoover does do that. But he also spends a considerable amount of time talking about his own activities, views, and reactions to the history that was then being made. To be sure, the name of Woodrow Wilson or the title president appears in nineteen of the twenty-one chapters in the book; but such chapters as "Woodrow Wilson's Administrative Ordeal in Paris" or "Woodrow Wilson's Ordeal of the Food Blockade on Europe" tend to push Wilson so far into the background that he becomes, in a sense, only the occasion for, rather than the subject of, such chapters—and Hoover takes over center stage. The pronoun "I," for example, appears over seventy-five times (excluding use in quoted letters) in the former chapter and about the same number of times in the latter.

Hoover, of course, had great admiration for Wilson; and it would be safe to assume that he was not simply using Wilson's experiences at the peace conference as an excuse to cover again his own activities there.[66] However, the book suffers to some degree because Hoover does not focus clearly and constantly enough on Wilson. A view of Hoover's own activities and responsibilities does add another dimension to those of Wilson, but it also tends to blur the main purpose of the book—that is, as Hoover stated, an understanding of Woodrow Wilson.

The strategy that Hoover follows in *The Ordeal of Woodrow Wilson* does succeed in presenting a starkly tragic picture of Wilson, who believed truly that what American soldiers died for in Europe transcended the obvious and immediate objects of the war and who struggled so valiantly, in both Europe and America, for his ideals of peace. Little doubt exists that Hoover *knew* Wilson and that the principles and ideals of the two were essentially identical. Edith Bolling Wilson, the wife of Woodrow Wilson, upon reading Hoover's book, wrote to him "that many people who have written about Mr. Wilson have been rather apologetic regarding what they term his 'stubbornness' but you seem to have really understood him."[67]

Nevertheless, *The Ordeal of Woodrow Wilson* does not succeed in really showing us Wilson the human being. As usual, Hoover's prose is spare and clear and simple; but what we get, as Luther Nichols remarked in a review in the *San Francisco Examiner*, "is a shadow picture of Wilson as an intellectual in a cannibal land full of hungry and emotional politicians."[68] Of course, in one sense, that is what Woodrow Wilson was.

CHAPTER 9

Prophet or Dreamer

IN looking back over the course of American history, it is possible and occasionally pertinent to point to some figures who, because they were conscious of the fateful logic with which history moves and because they were quick to grasp the quintessence of their times, are said to be symbols of an age. Benjamin Franklin and Andrew Jackson are two who come readily to mind. To say that Herbert Hoover could be seen as a symbol of an age might well cause many to raise their eyebrows or, taking another tack, to agree heartily that he was indeed a symbol of an age—the Age of Depression. Nevertheless, Hoover is very much a reflection of an age—not, to be sure, the age which he lived through, nor even an age that can be bracketed neatly by dates. On the contrary, he is a symbol of an age that itself exists only symbolically—the Age of the American Dream, a timeless age that had its beginning when the first explorers set foot upon a virgin continent and realized the material and spiritual prospects that lay before them—an age that has continued even to the present.

The American Dream has always manifested the duality of the material and the spiritual—a power aspect and an ideal aspect, which, at the same time that they have been carefully (and sometimes not so carefully) woven together, have often stood in conflict with each other. One version of this conflict arises from the effort to reconcile the democratic ideal of a nation founded on a concept of natural rights with the basic selfishness of man, a selfishness that in its own way was instrumental in the material development of that nation.

This development of America as a nation—at least up to the twentieth century—was based on four concepts: (1) an agrarian way of life, (2) cosmic optimism, (3) individualism, and (4)

153

progress and perfectibility. These concepts were undergirded by the Protestant ethic, which held that the worth of any man, either in the eyes of his fellows or of God, was in direct correlation to his capacity to be a self-reliant man of action who could win out over adversity. It is not by accident that American heroes have been primarily men of enterprise—Daniel Boone, Johnny Appleseed, Davy Crockett, Paul Bunyan, Andrew Carnegie, the log-cabin presidents.

Nor was it by accident that Herbert Hoover, when he returned from Europe in 1919 to carry on his career of public service, was seen by many as such a hero, a man of ability and enterprise. Born in the rural Midwest, reared there and in the West, educated in a new university—he had gone on to become one of the most successful and respected mining engineers of the world and one of the great humanitarians of that same world when it was ravaged by war. The fact that he was to become the victim of one of history's cruel ironies does not negate what Hoover represented. Indeed, it underscores what he represented.

Hoover, by the life he lived and by the life view he held, reflected the concepts mentioned above. While his agrarian experience came early and was shortlived, he was never out of touch with those values that marked the agrarian life. His optimism, moreover, was never dimmed, not even in his own darkest political days. And his belief in individualism and in the progress and perfectibility of America was expressed in virtually everything that he ever wrote or said. His Quakerism added a more spiritual dimension to the Protestant ethic and enabled him to blend the practical and the ideal into a smooth philosophical mix, seasoned with a kind of mystical patriotism based on distinct elements of the past. "He remains," according to Eugene Lyons, "an individualist of a peculiarly American brand and an uncompromising partisan of personal freedom—not because that's the middle of the road but because for him it is the whole road, the American road."[1]

Even his physical appearance, as described by Edward Eyre Hunt, one of his aides during the Commerce years, was that of the typical American—"the serious, effective, hard-driving business type which is known for an American from Greenland to Guam. His face is full, smooth shaven, his brow is wide. . .his eyes are quiet and keen, nose good, mouth strong, and chin strongest of all. . . . Every feature shows the thinker and doer.

His is an imaginative face, full of sentiment. Hoover is preeminently a man of ideals."[2]

Hoover rose to his zenith of political prominence in the 1920s, a decade that has been talked about and written about by sociologists, economists, political scientists, historians, and novelists and poets. Images of the 1920s abound, none of which alone sufficiently reflects the period—bootleggers, flappers, raccoon coats, Stutz Bearcats, jazz bands, iconoclastic writers. Rod Horton and Herbert Edwards pointed to the popular attitude that "holds that the age constituted a sort of screwball revue, a Marx Brothers extravaganza with a frenetic jazz orchestra in the pit and a bawdy farce on the stage, played amidst the artillery fire of gang wars, illicit champagne corks, and firecrackers placed under the chairs of old ladies from Dubuque."[3]

Picturesque as such a description is, it is not accurate. The 1920s were, as Horton and Edwards went on to say, "the beginning of a cycle of stress, a testing period to determine whether the long-cherished ideals of democracy, progress, and opportunity will continue as the motivating forces in American life, or whether our destinies will henceforth be controlled by some new, uncharacteristic, and more frankly cynical system."[4] In that sense, the 1920s were really a prelude to the 1930s—a decade that Hoover certainly saw as even more of a testing period than the previous one: "The outstanding State of this Union at this hour," he said in 1936, "is a state of confusion. Confusion in thought, confusion in government, confusion in economic life, and confusion in ideals."[5]

From the moment that Hoover left the White House, he carried on the battle against those forces that he perceived as cutting at the very roots of the American system. He was not willing to accept as an alternative a "more frankly cynical system." He was not willing to give up his belief in America and in Americans. "The word 'America,' " he said in 1940, "has always meant to me more than a land with political and economic systems of liberty. There is an imponderable in the word 'America' which calls to something far bigger and greater than that. Being of the spirit of a people it is indefinable."[6]

Because of this strong belief in America, Hoover gave no credence to such iconoclasts as Sinclair Lewis, resenting their criticisms of the stature and character of the American. "More particularly," he said, "I have resented the sneers at Main Street. For I have known that in the cottages that lay behind the street rested the strength of our national character."[7] Though he believed in the abstract notion of the perfectibility of America, Hoover was not a perfectionist. He also knew that some people were good and some were not. Both his mining and political experiences taught him that much.

It was his belief in America and in the American System, however, that underlay his political theory. Unlike Thomas Jefferson, he had a system; he was consistent. His words and his actions show the same thing. What he said, he believed, and what he believed, he did. Throughout all the writings and speeches that we have examined, Hoover rephrased and reiterated his basic ideas with a consistency and a simplicity. Not theoretical or fanciful, he glanced off abstractions and cut through ambiguities. If Jefferson held that individual liberty was best secured by the least possible government, Hoover held that individual opportunity was best secured by much government having a constant principle as its guide in legislation and administration.

Hoover saw government as having a sacred obligation to permit and encourage every individual to respond to the creative force within him. He firmly believed that every individual had an inherent yearning for self-expression. The nation, moreover, was in constant need of creative minds. Because each generation produced only a few truly creative minds and because progress depended upon them, they must be allowed to emerge from the mass. They must be allowed to be "uncommon." Such for Hoover was true liberalism.

Yet he saw true liberalism as going beyond that basic tenet of equality of opportunity. It was an attitude of mind. Speaking of it at Earlham College in 1938, he said,

Liberalism holds for the dignity of the individual man and woman. It insists that liberty lives by faith in the decency of average human nature. It seeks to create free men. It seeks all freedom to men that does not transgress the liberty of others. It rejects tyranny, whether bureaucratic or economic. Its purpose is not to extend bureaucracy but to set bounds to it. It holds to freedom of enterprise but that exploitation or monopoly is economic tyranny. It holds against every form of coercion of men of good will. It seeks this freedom in the confident belief that without such freedom the pursuit of other blessings is in vain. Real liberalism believes that truth, tolerance, mercy and human brotherhood are the roads to human understanding. It insists that all human advancement comes alone from free minds and free spirit. It keeps an open mind to any experiment that would promote those ends. It is born of liberty and cleaving to it makes the development of the highest form of human society. That is pure liberalism.[8]

Hoover never once doubted that the American economic and social system could cure whatever abuses grew out of it. This confidence in the essential self-healing character of that system was not that of a dreamer. Hoover knew well enough the difficulties that the modern world in all of its complexities could throw up as obstacles. "The advancement of science," he noted in a speech in 1924, "and our increasing population require constantly new standards of conduct and breed an increasing multitude of new rules and regulations. The basic principles laid down in the Ten Commandments and the Sermon on the Mount are as applicable today as when they were declared, but they require a host of subsidiary clauses. The ten ways to evil in the time of Moses have increased to ten thousand now."[9] Even so, Hoover would not accept the view that the conflicts generated by the Machine Age necessitated the sacrifice of the principles of liberty. To him, those principles were undying and just as workable in the Machine Age as in any previous age.

Hoover believed that commerce and industry could not eliminate abuses purely on a voluntary basis; there was need for regulation. Voluntary forces were, nevertheless, a vital component of the American System; for law and regulation do not in themselves build national character. Such character is the sum total of the moral fiber of the individuals that make up the nation. "The Union has become not merely a physical union of States," he said in 1930, "but rather is a spiritual union in common ideals of our people. Within it is room for every variety of opinion, every possibility of experiment in social progress. Out of such variety comes growth, but only as we preserve and maintain our spiritual solidarity."[10]

Cooperation among individuals, then, not coercion by government was to Hoover a key to problem solving at all levels. In this sense, he was caught in a conflict between the ideal world he so strongly believed in and the actual world which his own

experiences kept thrusting at him. And as he himself more
clearly came to recognize the cogency of this conflict, he more
fervently held to those virtues that he thought were badly
slipping in American life. Speaking in Des Moines in 1951, he
said,

> The practical thing we can do if we really want to make the world
> over again is to try out the word "old" for awhile. There are some "old"
> things that made this country.
> There is the Old Virtue of religious faith.
> There are the Old Virtues of integrity and the whole truth.
> There is the Old Virtue of incorruptible service and honor in public
> office.
> There are the Old Virtues of economy in government, of self-
> reliance, thrift, and individual liberty.
> There are the Old Virtues of patriotism, real love of country, and
> willingness to sacrifice for it.[11]

We might lament the fact that Herbert Hoover was not
possessed of a personal magnetism that could have reached
beyond the circle of close associates to provide a cadence that
the nation as a whole might have marched to. Nevertheless,
every task that Hoover set himself to, he did so with the utmost
seriousness of purpose, directing his considerable organizational
talent toward realizing his earnest wish to see the action of life
worked out and fitted together after a pattern that would result
in a maximum of human advancement. That he left the White
House a tragic figure—a victim of forces beyond his control—
does not diminish the essential integrity of his life view. The
philosophy that he championed may have been administered the
coup de grace by the New Deal, but it echoes and reechoes as
America, along with the rest of the world, moves dizzily through
the chaos of the twentieth century, beset by a plethora of social,
political, and economic problems that seem beyond the ken of
the superbureaucracy our government has become. "Why have
we not listened to the prophetic voice of Herbert Hoover?"
wrote Harold Chase in 1951. "Why have we allowed ourselves to
be swayed by the sirens' calls, voicing a false liberalism. . . . Mr.
Hoover, sitting on an Olympian height, saw it all in the making.
He warned us, but we were deaf to his pleadings."[12]
Herbert Hoover was both prophet and dreamer. Just as

Jefferson foresaw that America would not long remain an idyllic agrarian nation, Hoover realized that his own concept of America and the American System was well on its way to becoming more like a Currier and Ives print than a living reality. Perspective, however, is achieved through both reality and myth—and in that sense Hoover was not willing to give up his optimistic belief in America. And also in that sense, his ideas are certainly worth revisiting.

Notes and References

Chapter One

1. Michel-Guillaume de Crevecoeur, "What Is an American?" in Philip Durham and Everett L. Jones, *The Frontier in American Literature* (New York, 1969), p. 21.

2. Herbert Hoover, *The Memoirs of Herbert Hoover* (New York, 1951-1952), I, 1. Hereafter referred to as *Memoirs.*

3. *Memoirs*, I, 5.

4. *Memoirs*, I, 6.

5. *Memoirs*, I, 8.

6. Eugene Lyons, *Our Unknown Ex-President* (Garden City, New York, 1949), pp. 66-67.

7. Ibid., p. 68.

8. Ibid., p. 69.

9. Herbert Hoover, *On Growing Up* (New York, 1962), p. 141.

10 *Memoirs*, I, 12.

11. Ibid.

12. Hoover, *On Growing Up*, pp. 150-51.

13. *Memoirs*, I, 14.

14. Will Irwin, *Herbert Hoover, A Reminiscent Biography* (New York), p. 67.

15. Catherine Owens Peare, *The Herbert Hoover Story* (New York, 1965), p. 36.

16. *Memoirs*, I, 21.

17. *Memoirs*, I, 24.

18. *Memoirs*, I, 26.

19. *Memoirs*, I, 32.

20. Herbert Hoover, letter home, August 5, 1897, Pre-Commerce Papers (Box 35—Subject), Hoover Presidential Library, West Branch, Iowa.

21. Irwin, p. 77.

22. Herbert Hoover, letter home, October 6, 1897, Pre-Commerce Papers (Box 35—Subject), Hoover Presidential Library, West Branch, Iowa.

23. Herbert Hoover, letter home, August 9, 1897, Pre-Commerce Papers (Box 35—Subject), Hoover Presidential Library, West Branch, Iowa.

24. Lyons, p. 27.

25. *Memoirs*, I, 67.

26. *Memoirs*, I, 75.

27. Ibid.

28. *Memoirs*, I, 77.

29. *Memoirs*, I, 100.

30. Herbert Hoover, *Principles of Mining* (New York, 1909), p. iii.

31. Ibid., p. 186.

32. *Memoirs*, I, 123.

33. *Memoirs*, I, 105.

34. Irwin, p. 135.

35. *Memoirs*, I, 156.

36. Reprint of sketch in the *World's Work* (April 1915), no page number, Pre-Commerce Papers (Box 5—Subject), Hoover Presidential Library, West Branch, Iowa.

37. *Memoirs*, I, 159.

38. *Memoirs*, I, 167.

39. *Memoirs*, I, 193.

40. *Memoirs*, I, 218.

41. *Memoirs*, I, 225.

42. *Memoirs*, I, 242.

43. *Memoirs*, I, 250.

44. Ibid.

45. *Memoirs*, I, 276-77.

46. *Memoirs*, I, 286.

47. *Memoirs*, I, 293.

48. *Memoirs*, I, 321.

49. *Memoirs*, I, 322.

50. Herbert Hoover, letter to Woodrow Wilson, June 6, 1919, in *Memoirs*, I, 323.

51. *Memoirs*, I, 348.

52. *Memoirs*, I, 432.

53. *Memoirs*, I, 433.

54. Herbert Hoover, memorandum to Woodrow Wilson, April 11, 1919, in *Memoirs*, I, 456.

55. Ibid., p. 457.

56. John Maynard Keynes, *The Economic Consequences of the Peace* (New York, 1919), p. 257.

57. *Memoirs*, I, 467.

Chapter Two

1. *Memoirs*, II, 2.

2. *Memoirs*, II, 5.

3. Herbert Hoover, address at the dedication of Warren Harding's tomb at Marion, Ohio, June 16, 1931, in *The State Papers and Other Public Writings of Herbert Hoover*, William Myers and Walter Newton, eds. (New York, 1934), p. 586. Hereafter cited as *State Papers*.

4. *Memoirs*, II, 55.

5. Herbert Hoover, statement, February 6, 1920. Draft in Pre-Commerce Papers (Box 6—Subject), Hoover Presidential Library, West Branch, Iowa.

6. *Memoirs*, II, 198.

7. *Memoirs*, II, 207.

8. Ibid.

9. *Memoirs*, II, 217.

10. Herbert Hoover, Inaugural Address, March 4, 1929, in *Memoirs*, II, 222.

11. *Memoirs*, II, 223.

12. Herbert Hoover, quoted in Eugene Lyons, *Herbert Hoover: A Biography* (New York, 1964), p. 246.

13. Herbert Hoover, address at Valley Forge, May 30, 1931, in *State Papers*, I, 570.

14. Herbert Hoover, address accepting Republican nomination for president, August 11, 1932, in *State Papers*, II, 252.

15. *Memoirs*, III, 104.

16. Ibid.

17. Thomas Barclay, interview, *Oral Histories* (Container 2), Hoover Presidential Library, West Branch, Iowa.

18. *Memoirs*, III, 226.

19. *Memoirs*, III, 344.

20. *Memoirs*, III, 350.

21. *Memoirs*, III, 345.

22. Herbert Hoover, address to Republican Convention, June 10, 1936, in Peare, p. 217.

23. Herbert Hoover, address to Republican Convention, June 25, 1940, in *Addresses Upon the American Road, 1940-1941*, p. 250.

24. Herbert Hoover, press statement, December 8, 1941, in *Addresses Upon the American Road, 1941-1945*, p. 3.

25. Herbert Hoover, quoted in Lyons, *Herbert Hoover, A Biography*, p. 372.

26. George D. Aiken, interview, *Oral Histories* (Container 1), Hoover Presidential Library, West Branch, Iowa.

Chapter Three

1. Edgar Rickard, letter to Howard J. Heinz, December 2, 1922, Commerce Papers (Box 25—Subject), Hoover Presidential Library, West Branch, Iowa.

2. Herbert Hoover, *American Individualism* (New York, 1922), p. 1.

3. Ibid.

4. Ibid., p. 2.

5. Ibid., p. 4.

6. Ibid., p. 5.

7. Ibid.

8. Ibid., p. 7.

9. Ibid., p. 9.

10. Ibid., p. 10.

11. Ibid., pp. 12–13.

12. Ibid., p. 26.

13. Ralph Waldo Emerson, "Self-Reliance," in *Complete Essays and Other Writings,* Tremaine McDowell, ed. (New York, 1940), p. 146.

14. Walt Whitman, "Democratic Vistas," in *Complete Poetry and Selected Prose,* James E. Miller, ed. (Boston, 1959), p. 463.

15. Hoover, *American Individualism,* p. 15.

16. Ibid., p. 16.

17. Ibid., p. 17.

18. Ibid., pp. 21–22.

19. Ibid., p. 32.

20. Ibid., p. 38.

21. Ibid., p. 40.

22. Ibid., p. 43.

23. Ibid., p. 45.

24. Ibid., p. 49.

25. Ibid., p. 51.

26. Ibid., p. 55.

27. Ibid., p. 60.

28. Ibid., p. 63.

29. Ibid., p. 66.

30. Ibid.

31. Ibid., pp. 68–69.

32. Ibid., p. 69.

33. Ibid., p. 70.

34. Ibid., p. 72.

35. See Stanley Coblentz, review, *New York Herald,* January 14, 1923.

36. "Hoover's New Federalism," *New York Times Book Review,* December 17, 1921, p. 1.

37. Alvin Winston, review, *New York Call,* January 28, 1923.

38. Frederick Jackson Turner, letter to Hoover, January 14, 1923, Commerce Papers (Box 27—Subject), Hoover Presidential Library, West Branch, Iowa.

39. Mario S. Saija, letter to Hoover, January 13, 1923, Commerce

Papers (Box 27—Subject), Hoover Presidential Library, West Branch, Iowa.

40. Letter to Hoover (signature illegible), July 7, 1923, Commerce Papers (Box 27—Subject), Hoover Presidential Library, West Branch, Iowa.

41. Don Beltram Mathieu, letter to Hoover, January 24, 1923, Commerce Papers (Box 27—Subject), Hoover Presidential Library, West Branch, Iowa.

42. Horace D. Taft, letter to Hoover, Februay 6, 1923, Commerce Papers (Box 27—Subject), Hoover Presidential Library, West Branch, Iowa.

43. Hugh E. Walters, letter to Hoover, July 4, 1924, Commerce Papers (Box 26—Subject), Hoover Presidential Library, West Branch, Iowa.

44. Review of *American Individualism, Weekly People*, March 17, 1923.

Chapter Four

1. Theodore Joslin, *Hoover Off the Record* (Garden City, New York, 1934), pp. 44-45.

2. Herbert Hoover, *The New Day* (Stanford, California, 1928), p. 10.

3. Ibid., p. 17.

4. Ibid., p. 30.

5. Ibid., p. 31.

6. Ibid., p. 52.

7. Ibid., p. 59.

8. Ibid., p. 64.

9. Ibid., p. 77.

10. Ibid., pp. 83-84.

11. Ibid., pp. 95-96.

12. Ibid., p. 144.

13. Ibid., p. 154.

14. Ibid. Hoover's use of "rugged individualism" here was probably unintentional. On other occasions he disavowed the term, feeling that it had connotations of selfishness and exploitation and did not, therefore, fit his ideas of American individualism.

15. Ibid., p. 157.

16. Ibid., p. 158.

17. Ibid., p. 163.

18. Ibid., pp. 175-76.

19. Ibid., p. 180.

20. Ibid., p. 181.

21. Ibid., p. 208.

22. Ann O'Hara McCormick, "The Dawn of the Hoover Era," *New York Times Magazine*, May 12, 1929, p. 16.

23. Herbert Hoover and Calvin Coolidge, *Campaign Speeches of 1932* (Garden City, New York, 1933), p. 3.

24. Roy V. Peel and Thomas W. Donnelly, *The 1932 Campaign, An Analysis* (New York, 1935), p. 180.

25. Hoover warned of American overexpansion and overspeculation during his tenure as Secretary of Commerce under Harding and Coolidge.

26. *Campaign Speeches of 1932*, p. 4.

27. Ibid.

28. Ibid., p. 34.

29. Ibid., pp. 34-35.

30. Ibid., p. 100.

31. Ibid., p. 108.

32. Ibid., p. 211.

33. Ibid., p. 245.

34. Ibid., p. 260.

35. Ibid., p. 269.

36. Ibid., p. 271.

37. Howard Runkel, *Hoover's Speeches During His Presidency* (Stanford, California, 1950), p. 117.

38. Ibid., pp. 86-87.

Chapter Five

1. Lyons, *Herbert Hoover, A Biography*, pp. 333-34.

2. Herbert Hoover, *Addresses Upon the American Road, 1933-1938* (New York, 1938), p. 40.

3. Harry Brown, "How Can Hoover Be Muzzled?" *Salt Lake Tribune*, June 23, 1935, pp. 1, 9.

4. Herbert Hoover, *The Challenge to Liberty* (New York, 1934), p. 1.

5. Ibid., p. 2.

6. Ibid., p. 3.

7. Ibid., p. 6.

8. Ibid., p. 7.

9. Ibid., pp. 8-9.

10. Ibid., p. 23.

11. Ibid.

12. Ibid., p. 26.

13. Ibid., p. 27.

14. Ibid.

15. Ibid.

16. Ibid., p. 30.

17. Hugh Gibson, letter to Lewis Einstein, June 21, 1928, Pre-Presidential Papers (Box 339—Individual), Hoover Presidential Library, West Branch, Iowa.

18. *The Challenge to Liberty*, p. 48.

19. Ibid., p. 54.

20. Ibid., pp. 57-58.

21. Ibid., p. 59.

22. Ibid., p. 65.

23. Ibid., p. 79.

24. Ibid., p. 85.

25. Ibid.

26. Ibid., p. 107.

27. Ibid., p. 106.

28. Ibid., p. 116.

29. Ibid., p. 134.

30. Ibid., p. 135.

31. Ibid., p. 139.

32. Ibid., p. 145.

33. Ibid., p. 149.

34. Ibid., p. 154.

35. Ibid.

36. Ibid., p. 170.

37. Ibid., p. 180.

38. Richard Hofstadter, *The American Political Tradition* (New York, 1957), p. 305.

39. *The Challenge to Liberty*, p. 182.

40. Ibid., p. 188.

41. Ibid., p. 193.

42. Ibid., p. 203.

43. Ibid., p. 175.

44. Herbert Hoover, *Addresses Upon the American Road, 1933-1938*, pp. 182-83.

45. William Allen White, review, *New Orleans Tribune*, September 30, 1934.

Chapter Six

1. Herbert Hoover, *State Papers*, II, 260-61.

2. Ibid., p. 260.

3. Herbert Hoover, *America's First Crusade* (New York, 1941), p. 1.

4. Ibid., pp. 2-3.

5. Ibid., p. 4.

6. Ibid., p. 9.

7. Lloyd George, quoted in *America's First Crusade*, p. 14.

8. Ibid., p. 29.
9. Ibid., p. 30.
10. Ibid., p. 31.
11. Ibid., p. 33.
12. Ibid., p. 39.
13. Ibid.
14. Ibid., p. 40.
15. Ibid., p. 41.
16. Ibid., p. 46.
17. Ibid., pp. 65–66.
18. Ibid., p. 71.
19. Ibid., p. 74.
20. Ibid., p. 76.
21. Ibid., p. 77.
22. Ibid., p. 78.
23. Ibid., p. 79.
24. Ibid., p. 81.
25. Herbert Hoover, letter to Whitney Darrow, December 6, 1941, Post-Presidential Papers (Box 93—Subject), Hoover Presidential Library, West Branch, Iowa.
26. Ibid.
27. Walter Mills, review, *New York Herald Tribune*, January 18, 1942.
28. Llewellyn White, review, *Chicago Sun*, January 10, 1942.
29. Boak Carter, review, *New York Mirror*, February 4, 1942.
30. Herbert Hoover, *Addresses Upon the American Road, 1938-1940* (New York, 1940), pp. 178-79.
31. Ibid., p. 179.
32. Herbert Hoover, *A Cause to Win* (New York, 1951), p. 8.
33. Ibid., p. 3.
34. Ibid., p. 11.
35. Herbert Hoover, *Addresses Upon the American Road, 1950-1955* (Stanford, California, 1955), p. 79.
36. Herbert Hoover, *40 Key Questions about Our Foreign Policy* (Scarsdale, New York, 1952), p. 17.
37. Ibid., p. 24.
38. Ibid., p. 25.
39. Ibid., p. 26.
40. Ibid., p. 39.
41. Ibid., p. 52.
42. Hoover, *A Cause to Win*, p. 27.
43. Ibid., p. 30.
44. Ibid., p. 31.

Chapter Seven

1. Herbert Hoover and Hugh Gibson, *The Problems of Lasting Peace* (Garden City, New York, 1943), p. 13.
2. Ibid., pp. 13–14.
3. Ibid., p. 14.
4. Ibid., p. 16.
5. Ibid., p. 17.
6. Ibid., p. 18.
7. Ibid., p. 19.
8. Ibid., p. 21.
9. See Henry Adams, *The Education of Henry Adams* (New York, 1918).
10. *The Problems of Lasting Peace*, pp. 44–45.
11. Ibid., p. 47.
12. Ibid.
13. Ibid., p. 58.
14. Ibid., p. 64.
15. Ibid.
16. Ibid.
17. Ibid., p. 69.
18. Ibid., p. 73. This conference was attended by representatives from twenty-six countries and produced three important conventions dealing with the settling of international disputes, the laws and customs of land war, and the adaptation of the principles of the Geneva Convention (1864) to maritime war. A second conference was held in 1907.
19. *The Problems of Lasting Peace*, p. 89.
20. Ibid., pp. 90–91.
21. Ibid., p. 105.
22. Ibid.
23. Ibid., p. 107.
24. Ibid., p. 109.
25. Ibid., p. 110.
26. Ibid., p. 118.
27. Ibid., p. 128.
28. Ibid., p. 132.
29. Ibid., pp. 136–37.
30. Herbert Hoover, quoted in Gary Dean Best, *The Politics of American Individualism* (Westport, Connecticut, 1975), p. 25.
31. *The Problems of Lasting Peace*, p. 145.
32. Ibid., p. 155.
33. Ibid., p. 202.

34. Hoover recommended in 1929 that during war the overseas food supply of all combatants should be vested in the hands of combined neutrals, to be delivered free from blockade and attack.

35. Herbert Hoover and Hugh Gibson, *The Basis of Lasting Peace* (New York, 1945), p. 11.

36. R. M. MacIver, review, *New York Times Book Review*, April 29, 1945, p. 1.

Chapter Eight

1. Herbert Hoover, *The Ordeal of Woodrow Wilson* (New York, 1958), p. vi.

2. Ibid.

3. Ibid., p. vii.

4. Ibid., p. viii.

5. Ibid., p. 2.

6. Ibid., p. 3.

7. Ibid., p. 7.

8. Frank Cobb, quoted in Hofstadter, *The American Political Tradition*, p. 271.

9. *The Ordeal of Woodrow Wilson*, p. 11.

10. Ibid.

11. Ibid., p. 13.

12. Hoover mentions Colonel House as one of Wilson's chief critics in his administration of the war. House urged Wilson to let him set up a war machine, since Wilson did not have the ability to do it.

13. *The Ordeal of Woodrow Wilson*, p. 15.

14. Ibid., p. 16.

15. Francis William O'Brien, *The Hoover-Wilson Wartime Correspondence* (Ames, Iowa, 1974), p. 283.

16. Herbert Hoover, *Memoirs*, I, 266.

17. *The Ordeal of Woodrow Wilson*, p. 17.

18. Ibid., p. 19.

19. Hoover tells us that Wilson had no speech writer, but composed the first draft of a speeh at his own typewriter, sometimes submitting it to colleagues for suggestions.

20. *The Ordeal of Woodrow Wilson*, pp. 20–22.

21. Ibid., p. 28.

22. Ibid.

23. Ibid., p. 41.

24. Ibid., p. 46.

25. Ibid., p. 60.

26. Hofstadter, p. 272.

27. *The Ordeal of Woodrow Wilson*, p. 61.

28. Ibid.

29. Ibid., p. 63.
30. Ibid., p. 64.
31. Ibid., p. 68.
32. Ibid., p. 73.
33. Ibid., p. 74.
34. Ibid., p. 77.
35. Ibid., p. 81.
36. Ibid., p. 87.
37. Ibid., p. 94.
38. Ibid., p. 101.
39. Ibid., pp. 115-16.
40. Ibid., p. 117.
41. Ibid., p. 119.
42. Ibid., p. 134.
43. Ibid., p. 151.
44. Ibid., p. 157.
45. Ibid., p. 180.
46. Ibid., p. 183.
47. Ibid., p. 186.
48. Ibid., p. 191.
49. Ibid., p. 193. Hoover here is quoting from the Papers of Charles L. Swem, Wilson's secretary, who took copious shorthand notes of the president's conversations.
50. Ibid., p. 196.
51. Ibid., pp. 197-98.
52. Ibid., p. 199.
53. Britain, France, and Italy signed in 1915 the Pact of London, which assured Italy certain territories if she were to enter the war.
54. *The Ordeal of Woodrow Wilson*, p. 206. The Italians did eventually return to the Peace Conference and did join the League of Nations.
55. These rights were formerly German rights and were promised to Japan by Britain and France in a secret treaty early in the war.
56. Ibid., pp. 217-18.
57. As a result of this compromise, over 16,000,000 people and over 1,000,000 square miles of territory were added to the empires of Britain, France, Italy, and Japan.
58. Ibid., p. 234.
59. Ibid., p. 248.
60. Ibid., p. 249.
61. Ibid.
62. Ibid., p. 263.
63. Ibid., p. 293.
64. Ibid., p. 295.
65. Ibid., pp. 300-301.

66. Hoover's experiences with the Food Blockade and the Belgian Relief are discussed in *Memoirs* and in *An American Epic*.

67. Edith Bolling Wilson, letter to Herbert Hoover, April 8, 1958, Post-Presidential Papers (Box 160—Subject), Hoover Presidential Library, West Branch, Iowa.

68. Luther Nichols, review, *San Francisco Examiner*, April 27, 1958.

Chapter Nine

1. Lyons, *Our Unknown Ex-President*, p. 18.

2. Edward Eyre Hunt, note in Pre-Commerce Papers (Box 6—Subject), Hoover Presidential Library, West Branch, Iowa.

3. Rod Horton and Herbert Edwards, *Backgrounds of American Literary Thought* (New York, 1967), p. 293.

4. Ibid., p. 295.

5. Herbert Hoover, *Addresses Upon the American Road, 1933–1938*, p. 115.

6. Herbert Hoover, *Addresses Upon the American Road, 1940–1941*, p. 53.

7. Herbert Hoover, *The New Day*, p. 109.

8. Herbert Hoover, *Addresses Upon the American Road, 1938–1940*, pp. 211–12.

9. Herbert Hoover, quoted in Wilbur and Hyde, p. 301.

10. Herbert Hoover, *State Papers*, I, 306.

11. Herbert Hoover, *Addresses Upon the American Road, 1950–1955*, p. 113.

12. Harold Chase, Worcester (Massachusetts) *Telegram*, October 14, 1951.

Selected Bibliography

This bibliography, both in its primary and secondary sources, is highly selective. Those interested in a complete listing of Herbert Hoover's writings and speeches are referred to Kathleen Tracey's *Herbert Hoover—A Bibliography: His Writings and Addresses.*

PRIMARY SOURCES

1. Books (chronologically listed)

Principles of Mining. New York: McGraw Hill Company, 1909.

With Lou Henry Hoover, joint translators. *Georgius Agricola de re Metallica.* New York: Dover Press, 1950 (a later edition).

American Individualism. Garden City, New York: Doubleday, Doran and Company, 1922.

The Challenge to Liberty. New York: Charles Scribner's Sons, 1934.

Shall We Send Our Youth to War? New York: Crowell-Collier, 1939.

America's First Crusade. New York: Charles Scribner's Sons, 1942.

With Hugh Gibson. *The Problems of Lasting Peace.* Garden City, New York: Doubleday, Doran and Company, 1942.

With Hugh Gibson. *The Basis of Lasting Peace.* New York: D. Van Nostrand, 1945.

The Memoirs of Herbert Hoover. Three volumes. New York: Macmillan Company, 1951-1952. Volume 1: *Years of Adventure, 1874-1920.* Volume 2: *The Cabinet and the Presidency, 1920-1933.* Volume 3: *The Great Depression, 1929-1941.*

The Ordeal of Woodrow Wilson. New York: McGraw Hill Company, 1958.

An American Epic. Four Volumes. Chicago: H. Regnery Company, 1959-1965. Volume 1: *The Relief of Belgium and Northern France, 1914-1923.* Volume 2: *Famine in Forty-Five Nations, Organization Behind the Front, 1914-1923.* Volume 3: *Famine in Forty-Five Nations, The Battle on the Front Line, 1914-1923.* Volume 4: *The Guns Cease Killing and the Saving of Life from Famine Begins, 1939-1963.*

Fishing for Fun and to Wash Your Soul. New York: Random House, 1963.

2. Collections (chronologically listed)

The New Day: Campaign Speeches of Herbert Hoover, 1928. Stanford,
  California: Stanford University Press, 1928.
A Boyhood in Iowa. New York: Aventine Press, 1931.
With Calvin Coolidge. *Campaign Speeches of 1932.* Garden City, New
  York: Doubleday, Doran and Company, 1933.
*Hoover After Dinner: Addresses Delivered by Herbert Hoover Before
  the Gridiron Club of Washington, D.C.* New York: Charles
  Scribner's Sons, 1933.
The State Papers and Other Public Writings of Herbert Hoover. Myers,
  William Starr, and Walter H. Newton, eds. Two Volumes. New
  York: Doubleday, Doran and Company, 1934.
*Public Papers of the President of the United States: Herbert Hoover,
  1929, 1930, and 1931.* Three Volumes. Washington D.C.: Office of
  the *Federal Register,* National Archives and Records Service, 1974
  and 1976. One volume forthcoming.
Addresses Upon the American Road, 1933-1938. New York: Charles
  Scribner's Sons, 1938.
Further Addresses Upon the American Road, 1938-1940. New York:
  Charles Scribner's Sons, 1940.
Addresses Upon the American Road, 1940-1941. New York: Charles
  Scribner's Sons, 1941.
Addresses Upon the American Road, World War II, 1941-1945. New
  York: D. Van Nostrand, 1946.
Addresses Upon the American Road, 1945-1948. New York: D. Van
  Nostrand, 1949.
Addresses Upon the American Road, 1948-1950. Stanford, California:
  Stanford University Press, 1951.
*A Cause to Win: Five Speeches by Herbert Hoover on American Foreign
  Policy in Relation to Soviet Russia.* New York: A Freeman
  Pamphlet, 1951.
Forty Key Questions About Our Foreign Policy. Scarsdale, New York:
  Updegraff Press, 1952.
Addresses Upon the American Road, 1950-1955. Stanford, California:
  Stanford University Press, 1955.
Addresses Upon the American Road, 1955-1960. Caldwell, Idaho:
  Caxton Printers, 1961.
On Growing Up. New York: William Morrow, 1962.

SECONDARY SOURCES

BEST, GARY DEAN. *The Politics of American Individualism.* Westport,
  Connecticut: Greenwood Press, 1975. A look at the interlude of

1918-1921, the period in Hoover's career when he began to articulate his philosophy of American individualism.

COREY, HERBERT. *The Truth about Hoover*. Boston: Houghton Mifflin, 1932. Purportedly an objective view of Hoover that, while not written chronologically, touches on many aspects of his life.

DEXTER, WALTER FRIAR. *Herbert Hoover and American Individualism*. New York: Macmillan Company, 1932. Good coverage of Hoover's ideas of American individualism as it relates to freedom, government, economics, and war.

DRESSLER, THOMAS. *The Foreign Policies of American Individualism*. Ann Arbor, Michigan: University Microfilms, 1973. An examination of Hoover's world-view as it influenced his foreign-policy decisions during his years as secretary of commerce and as president.

FAUSOLD, MARTIN, and GEORGE. MAZUZAN, *The Hoover Presidency: A Reappraisal*. Albany, New York: State University of New York Press, 1974. An attempt to present a more complete perspective on Hoover's foreign policy through a number of scholarly interpretations. A good single source.

HINSHAW, DAVID. "Friends of the Truth," *Century* 120 (Spring 1930): 227-35. An attempt to dispell erroneous ideas regarding Quakers and to see Hoover's approach to the handling of problems in light of his Quaker background.

HOFSTADTER, RICHARD. *The American Political Tradition*. New York: Alfred Knopf, 1948. Contains excellent chapters on Hoover, Wilson, and Franklin Roosevelt, among others.

IRWIN, WILL. *Herbert Hoover, A Reminiscent Biography*. New York: The Century Company, 1928. A pro-Hoover biography covering the years prior to his election to the presidency.

JOSLIN, THEODORE. *Hoover Off the Record*. New York: Doubleday, Doran and Company, 1934. A valuable and interesting firsthand record of Hoover's administration by his secretary (1931-1933).

KELLOG, VERNON. *Herbert Hoover: The Man and His Work*. New York: D. Appleton and Company, 1920. An early biographical study of Hoover by a critic of social Darwinism.

KEYNES, JOHN MAYNARD. *The Economic Consequences of the Peace*. New York: Charles Scribner's Sons, 1919. A discussion of the Treaty of Versailles and the economic implications it held for the world. Good for a comparison with Hoover's ideas.

KROCK, ARTHUR. *Memoirs*. New York: Fuk and Wagnalls, 1968. A book that contains chapters on a number of American presidents of the twentieth century—including a cryptic but interesting one on Hoover.

LAMONT, ROBERT PATTERSON. "The Personality of President Hoover," *Review of Reviews* 86 (September 1932): 23-25. An attempt to dispel the impression that Hoover was a rigid personality lacking real feeling.

LANE, ROSE WILDER. *The Making of Herbert Hoover.* New York: The Century Company, 1920. A kind of dramatization of Hoover's career from the beginnings through his work with the Belgian Relief.

LLOYD, CRAIG. *Aggressive Introvert.* Columbus: Ohio State University Press, 1972. An analysis of the behind-the-scenes public-relations techniques that Hoover utilized in his efforts to influence men and events. Well documented.

LYONS, EUGENE. *Our Unknown Ex-President.* Garden City, New York: Doubleday and Company, 1949. An informative biography of Hoover that attempts to dispell the myth of Hoover as a heartless ogre who caused the depression.

———. *Herbert Hoover, A Biography.* Garden City, New York: Doubleday and Company, 1964. A friendly biography that includes materials from Lyons' first book and goes on to cover Hoover's entire career.

MYERS, WILLIAM S., and WALTER H. NEWTON, *The Hoover Administration, A Documented Narrative.* New York: Charles Scribner's Sons, 1936. A discussion of the policies and activities of the Hoover administration—with considerable documentation from primary sources.

NELSON, CLAIR EVERET. *The Image of Herbert Hoover as Reflected in the American Press.* Unpublished Dissertation. Stanford University, 1956. A thorough analysis of the treatment given Hoover by the daily and periodical press of the United States.

O'BRIEN, FRANCIS WILLIAM. *The Hoover-Wilson Wartime Correspondence.* Ames: Iowa State University Press, 1974. Coverage of the correspondence between Hoover and Woodrow Wilson during World War I with valuable commentary by the author.

PEARE, CATHERINE. *The Herbert Hoover Story.* New York: Thomas Crowell Company, 1965. A readable storybook biography of Hoover that is very positive in approach.

PEEL, ROY V., and DONNELLY, THOMAS C. *The 1928 Campaign.* New York: Richard R. Smith, 1931. An informative, though often biased, discussion of the issues of the 1928 presidential campaign and the personalities of the candidates—Hoover and Smith.

———. *The 1932 Campaign: An Analysis.* New York: J. J. Little and Ives, 1935. Same format as the previous work.

PENNIMAN, HOWARD. *Sait's American Parties and Elections,* fifth edition. New York: Appleton-Century-Crofts, 1952. No extensive discussion of Hoover but good insight into American political parties and elections.

RICE, ARNOLD, ed. *Herbert Hoover 1874-1964.* Dobbs Ferry, New York: Oceana Publications, 1971. A valuable compilation of chronological, documentary, and bibliographical aids regarding Hoover.

RICHELSON, JOHN. "Herbert Hoover and the Quakers," *Current History* 30 (April 1929): 79-83. Speculation on the Quaker influences on Hoover's life view and on his actions.

ROBINSON, EUGENE, and BORNET, VAUGHAN. *Herbert Hoover, President of the United States.* Stanford, California: Hoover Institution Press, 1975. An analysis of the four years of Hoover's administration, presenting Hoover as a man who believed in, and held to, certain basic principles.

RUNKEL, HOWARD WILLIAM. *Hoover's Speeches during His Presidency.* Unpublished Dissertation. Stanford University, 1950. A detailed study of the structure and content of Hoover's presidential speeches.

SLOSSON, PRESTON W. *The Great Crusade and After: 1914-1928.* Volume XII of *A History of American Life,* Arthur Schlessinger and Dixon Fox, eds. New York: The Macmillan Company, 1930. Informative survey of the period in which Hoover rose to prominence.

SMITH, FRANCIS WILSON. *Herbert Hoover's "American Individualism" in the History of American Thought.* Unpublished Thesis. University of California-Berkeley, 1948. A study of *American Individualism* as an approach to a broader survey of Hoover's political and economic philosophy.

SMITH, GENE. *The Shattered Dream.* New York: William Morrow and Company, 1970. Coverage of Hoover's administration and the demise of the American dream of rugged individualism and of Roosevelt's first administration as it symbolized a new kind of dream.

SMITH, T. V. *The American Philosophy of Equality.* Chicago: University of Chicago Press, 1927. A comprehensive view of the sources and characteristics of the American concept of equality. Valuable as a backdrop for Hoover's own ideas of equality.

TRACEY, KATHLEEN. *Herbert Hoover—A Bibliography.* Stanford, California: Hoover Institution Press, 1977. A listing of virtually every item that Hoover wrote and every speech that he gave. An invaluable research tool.

WILBUR, RAY LYMAN, and HYDE, ARTHUR. *The Hoover Policies.* New York: Charles Scribner's Sons, 1937. A documentary description of Hoover's policies and principles in action during his administration.

WOLFE, HAROLD. *Herbert Hoover, Public Servant and Leader of the Loyal Opposition.* New York: Exposition Press, 1956. Coverage of Hoover's life, with major emphasis on his public career and activities and some attention to personal items.

Woodward, Walter. "The Individual and the State," in S. B. Laughlin, ed., *Beyond Dilemmas: Quakers Look at Life*. Philadelphia: J. B. Lippincott Company, 1937. An informative article on the Quaker view of the individual's relationship to government that provides good insight into Hoover's ideas.

Index

179